Skills in English

Listening .Level 3

Contents

KT-161-307

Book Map

Theme	Listening text type	Aural skills
1 **Education,** How Do We Learn?	Lecture	• Revision
2 **Daily Life,** Growing Up	Lecture	• Fixed phrases • Using abbreviations in notes • Taking notes of stories, ideas, etc.
3 **Work and Business,** Why Do People Work Hard?	Lecture	• Using symbols in notes • Recognising digressions
4 **Science and Nature,** Tornadoes and Hurricanes	Talk	• Signposts – reminders • Mini-signposts • Leaving space in notes for missing information
5 **The Physical World,** Natural Disasters	Lecture	• Rhetorical questions • Two-sided signposts
6 **Culture and Civilization,** What Is Society?	Lecture	• Distinguishing fact from opinion • Participating in discussions
7 **They Made Our World,** The Greatest Advance in History	Talk	• Understanding a speaker's argument
8 **Art and Literature,** Gulliver and Robinson Crusoe	Talk	• Guessing the spelling of proper nouns • Understanding dramatic language
9 **Sports and Leisure,** $5,000,000,000,000 p.a.	Lecture with questions	• Understanding pros and cons • Contributing to discussions
10 **Nutrition and Health,** Food – The New Poison?	Lecture with questions	• Revision

Skills in English

Level 3

Listening

Terry Phillips

Published by
Garnet Publishing Ltd.
8 Southern Court
South Street
Reading RG1 4QS, UK

Copyright © 2004 Garnet Publishing Ltd.

The right of Terry Phillips to be identified as the author of this work has been asserted by him in accordance with the Copyright, Designs and Patents Act 1988.

All rights reserved.
No part of this publication may be reproduced, stored in a retrieval system, or transmitted in any form or by any means, electronic, mechanical, photocopying, recording or otherwise, without the prior permission of the Publisher. Any person who does any unauthorized act in relation to this publication may be liable to criminal prosecution and civil claims for damages.

This edition first published 2004

ISBN 1 85964 790 1

British Library Cataloguing-in-Publication Data
A catalogue record for this book is available from the British Library.

Production

Project manager:	Richard Peacock
Editorial team:	Nicky Platt, Lucy Thompson
Art director:	David Rose
Design:	Mark Slader
Illustration:	Beehive Illustration/Simon Rumble/ RogerWade-Walker, Janette Hill, Karen Rose
Photography:	Corbis, Digital Vision, Mary Evans Picture Library, NOAA Photo Library, Photodisc

Every effort has been made to trace the copyright holders and we apologize in advance for any unintentional omissions. We will be happy to insert the appropriate acknowledgements in any subsequent editions.

Audio production: Matinée Sound & Vision Ltd.

Printed and bound
in Lebanon by International Press

Introduction

THIS COURSE IS THE LISTENING COMPONENT of Level 3 of the *Skills in English* series. The series takes students in four levels from Lower Intermediate to Advanced in the four skills, Listening, Speaking, Reading and Writing.

The listening component at each level is designed to build skills that help students survive in an academic institution where lectures are wholly or partly in English.

This component can be studied on its own or with one or more of the other components, e.g., Speaking and Reading.

The course is organised into themes, e.g., *Science and Nature, Art and Literature*. The same theme is used across the four skills. If, therefore, you are studying two or more components, the vocabulary and structures that you learn or practise in one component will be useful in another component.

Within each theme there are four lessons:

Lesson 1: *Vocabulary*
In the first lesson, you revise words from the theme that you have probably learnt already. You also learn some new words that you need to understand the texts in the rest of the theme.

Lesson 2: *Listening*
In this lesson, you practise skills that you have learnt in previous themes.

Lesson 3: *Learning new skills*
In this lesson, you learn one or more new skills to help you with listening.

Lesson 4: *Applying new skills*
In the final lesson, you use your new skills with another listening text. In most cases, the texts in Lessons 2 and 4 have a similar structure, so you can check that your skills have improved.

In this theme you are going to listen to a lecture on theories of learning.

Lesson 1: Vocabulary

You are going to learn some of the vocabulary you will need to understand the lecture.

A Discuss these questions in pairs. They use some of the red words.
1 Do you have a good *memory*?
2 Which of these do you find it easy to *remember*?
   ☐ names
   ☐ telephone numbers
   ☐ faces
   ☐ interesting facts
   ☐ jokes
3 What makes a new word in English *memorable* for you?
4 Do you ever *forget* important things? When did you last *forget* something important?

B 📼 Listen to a short text with the green words. Then complete the text with one of the words in each space.

What is _____? Scientists define learning as a change of _____. But how do we learn? Nobody knows for sure, but there are many _____ from psychologists and philosophers. Some say, 'People learn from _____. For example, a baby cries and his mother gives him food. He learns that certain _____ is useful.' Other people think that we learn by _____. They say, 'We look around at the world. We _____ other people. We see how they _____. We copy them.'

C Discuss these questions in groups.
1 Do you think a baby learns from experience, observation or another way?
2 What about an adult?

D What are the strong sounds in the green words?
1 Mark the strong sound in each word.
2 📼 Listen and number the words you hear.

---

forget *(v)*

memorable *(adj)*

memory *(n)*

remember *(v)*

behave *(v)*

behaviour *(n)*

experience *(n)*

learning *(n)*

observation *(n)*

observe *(v)*

theory/ies *(n)*

Lesson 2: Listening

A How can you teach a child each of these things?
  • to ride a bicycle
  • that hot things burn you
  • 6 multiplied by 7 is 42
  • to be kind to people

B You are going to hear a lecture about learning.
  1 Read the Skills Check Reminder.
  2 📼 Listen to the introduction. Complete the outline.
  3 Which of these sentences do you expect to hear in this week's lecture?
  a A common theme in Islamic science is that learning comes from studying nature.
  b Pavlov's experiment led to a new theory about human learning.
  c Russia has a population of more than 145 million.
  d The Greek philosopher Plato lived from 427 BCE to about 347 BCE.
  e Today we're going to learn about Ancient Greece.

C 📼 Listen to the first part of the lecture.
  1 What are the important pieces of information here?
  Example: *the person*
  2 Complete the first row of Table 1 below. Write one word in each place.
  3 Complete the second row with information about the first person.

D 📼 Listen to the rest of the lecture. Complete Table 1.

E Do we learn different things in different ways? Look back at Exercise A. Can you match each piece of knowledge with one of the theories in Table 1?

Skills Check

Reminder

When you listen to a lecture, you must …
  1 understand the signpost words in the introduction – they tell you the structure of the lecture.
  2 predict the content – then listen and check.
  3 identify the important information – make notes in an outline or a table.

How do we _____?
Lecture 1:
1. Ancient _____
2. _____ scholars
3. _____

Lecture 2:
1. Skinner
2. Watson

Table 1: Theories of learning

person	period		theory	
Plato		Greece		child touches fire, burns himself, learns not to touch fire

Lesson 3: Checking skills

A In this lesson, you are going to practise some more listening skills.
1 Read the Skills Check Reminder.
2 Close your book. Make a list of things you must do when you listen to a lecture.
3 Compare your list with the Skills Check.

B Can you understand the main ideas in a lecture?
1 Match the people to their theories.
2 What example did the lecturer give for each theory?

    a Plato   **1** We learn by observing.
    b Aristotle   **2** We learn by remembering.
    c Islamic scholars   **3** We learn by understanding why.
    d Pavlov   **4** We learn through conditioning.

C Can you predict the order of information in a lecture?
1 Read the section from the lecture in Lesson 2 in the pink box. Make a list of the different pieces of information here.
2 The next section is about Aristotle. What information do you expect to hear? In what order?
3 🔘 Listen and check your ideas.

D Can you understand the sequence of events in a lecture?
1 The sentences in the yellow box tell the story of Pavlov's famous experiment. Number them in order.
2 🔘 Listen and check.

    a After a short time, the dog salivated when it heard the bell, without getting the food.
    b After a short time, the dog stopped salivating when it heard the bell.
    c Every time the dog licked the powder, Pavlov rang a bell.
    d He gave a dog some meat powder every few minutes.
    e He rang a bell but didn't give the dog any food.
    f He reversed the experiment.

E Can you identify words in a lecture from the strong sounds?
1 Complete the long words from sections of the lecture.
2 🔘 Listen and check.

F How do you learn English? Do you use any of the ways mentioned in the lecture?

Skills Check

Reminder

When you listen to a lecture, you must …
1 **understand the main ideas** – who, what, when, where?
2 **predict the order of information** – then listen and check.
3 **understand the sequence of events** – in what order did the events happen?
4 **identify important words** – from the strong sounds.

The Greek philosopher Plato – that's P-L-A-T-O – lived from 427 BCE to about 347 BCE. He believed that learning was just memory. We have an experience. Maybe it's good. Maybe it's bad. Maybe we remember. Maybe we forget. If we remember later, that's learning by experience. For example, a child touches a fire and burns himself. He remembers next time and doesn't touch the fire.

What is the <u>connection</u> <u>be</u>tween Pavlov's dogs and hu___ lear_____? Pavlov's ___pe_____ led to a new the_____ about how we learn. Scien_____ said that ___vents in our ___vi_____ can change the way we ___have. Pavlov called this pro_____ '_____di_____'. Pavlov's the_____ says a child can ___come fright_____ of some_____ _____out having di____ ___pe_____ and _____out _____ser_____ some_____ else having the _____pe_____.

Lesson 4: Applying skills

A Here are the examples from the lecture in Lessons 2 and 3. Which theory of learning does each one support?

1

A child touches a fire and burns himself.
He remembers next time.
He doesn't touch the fire.

3

A child observes another child touching a fire.
He sees that the other child is burnt.
He does not touch the fire himself.

2

A child touches a fire and burns himself.
Later he touches a match and burns himself.
He sees a pattern: hot things burn you.
After the child sees the pattern, he does not touch any hot things, including irons and boiling water – things that haven't burnt him in the past.

4

A mother sees her child is going to touch a fire.
She shouts, 'No!'
She frightens the child.
The child connects the fear and the fire, even though he did not get burnt himself or see anyone else getting burnt.

B You are going to hear the second lecture on theories of learning.
  1 What did the lecturer say about this lecture?
  2 🔊 Listen to the introduction. Make outline notes for the lecture.

C 🔊 Listen to the first part of the lecture. What is the main point of this part?
Tick (✔) one of the following.
  __ Watson did experiments with a baby and a rat.
  __ Watson proved that Pavlov's conditioning works with people as well as animals.
  __ Watson believed that people's experiences are very important.
  __ Albert cried every time the rat appeared.

D 🔊 Listen to the second part of the lecture. Connect the pictures and explain the main ideas in this part.

E 🔊 Listen to the third part of the lecture. Number these events in order.
  __ Her baby makes a sound.
  __ The baby says 'Mummy' when his mother comes into the room.
  __ A mother comes into a room.
  __ The mother says 'Mummy'.
  __ The mother thinks: 'That sounds like the word *Mummy*.'
  __ The same thing happens hundreds of times.

F What is the connection between Skinner's work and language learning?

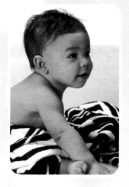

In this theme you are going to hear two lectures about child development.

Lesson 1: Vocabulary

You are going to learn some of the vocabulary you will need to understand the lectures.

(A) Discuss these questions in pairs. They use some of the red words.
1 Should you always accept the *behaviour* of your friends?
2 When did you last *criticise* someone? What did you say?
3 Are you an *optimistic* person? What is your *attitude* towards the future?
4 Should you *trust* people when you meet them for the first time?
5 Are your best friends from your *neighbourhood*, or are they *colleagues* at college or university?

(B) 🔊 Listen to a short text with the green words. Then complete the text with one of the words in each space. Make any necessary changes.

Do you sometimes ask yourself: 'Who am I?' If you do, you are normal. Indeed, psychologists say that we ask ourselves this question throughout our lives. The meaning of the question changes as we _____ _____. _____ ask, 'Who am I? Is this hand part of me, or part of you?' _____ ask, 'Who am I? My parents choose my clothes, my food, my school, my bedtime.' _____ ask, 'Who am I? A nice person or a nasty one?' _____ adults ask, 'Who am I? What have I done with my life?'

   We ask the question because, according to Erik Erikson (see Lesson 4), at every age there is an _____ crisis – a _____ or battle between who we are and who we would like to be. At every age we find different answers, because, according to Piaget (see Lesson 2), our brains develop in a predictable way through _____ and _____ to _____.

(C) There is a logical relationship between the words and phrases in the blue box.
1 Number them in a logical order.
2 🔊 Listen and check your ideas.

> adolescence adulthood birth
> childhood death infancy middle age

(D) What is the relationship between *infant* and *infancy*? Find other pairs of words with the same relationship.

(E) There are three theories in the text in Exercise B.
1 Find and underline them. Explain the theories in your own words.
2 Do you agree with them? Why (not)?

accept *(v)*

attitude *(n)*

behaviour *(n)*

colleague *(n)*

criticise *(v)*

neighbourhood *(n)*

occasion *(n)*

optimistic *(adj)*

trust *(v)*

adolescence *(n)*

adolescent *(n)*

adulthood *(n)*

baby *(n)*

conflict *(n)*

develop *(v)*

grow up *(v)*

identity *(n)*

infancy *(n)*

infant *(n)*

middle-aged *(adj)*

Lesson 2: Listening

A Read the information on the college leaflet. What do you think the lecturer will talk about in ...
  1 the first lecture?
  2 the second lecture?

B 📼 Listen to the introduction. Make a set of outline notes for this week's lecture.

C Think about the first part of this week's lecture.
  1 Make a list of possible words.
  2 What is the best way to record the information?

D Work in pairs.
  1 📼 Listen to the first part of the lecture.

| **Student A** | **Student B** |
| Make notes on the events in Piaget's life. | Make notes on Piaget's work and ideas. |

  2 Exchange information.
  3 📼 Listen again. Put the notes on Piaget's life, work and ideas together.

E 📼 Listen to the second part of the lecture.
  1 What was the first experiment?
  2 What was the second experiment?
  3 What does each experiment show about child development?
  4 How many stages of child development did Piaget identify?

F Look at some of the learning tasks in the yellow box. At what stage do children learn each of these things?
  1 Write 1, 2, 3 or 4 in front of each point.
  2 📼 Listen to the third part of the lecture and check your ideas.

___ If I do this, this will happen.
___ What things feel like, sound like, etc.
___ A litre of water is the same in a big bottle or a small one.
___ Speech
___ Abstract ideas like algebra
___ Past and future

G 📼 Listen to the third part again. Complete the table.

Table 1: Piaget's stages of child development

stage	age range	name of stage	development / learning
1	*birth–1.5/2 yrs*	*Sensorimotor*	
2	*7 yrs–12 yrs*	*Pre-operational thought*	
3		*Concrete operational thought*	*real things stay the same*
4			*algebra, hypotheses, abstract ideas*

Greenhill College leaflet:

Greenhill College

Faculty: Sociology   Semester 3

Topic: Child Development

There are two lectures on this topic. In these lectures, we are going to look at two theories of child development, from infancy to adolescence. Before you attend the lectures, please do some research on:

• Jean Piaget
• Erik Erikson

Lesson 3: Learning new skills

A Some toys and games are only suitable for particular age groups. Can you explain why? (Clue: Piaget's stages)

B We have seen many fixed phrases in this course (e.g., Level 2 Theme 2).

  1 Read Skills Check 1.

  2 Find a word in the right column to complete each phrase.

  3 🎧 Listen and check your ideas.

a	cause and	**1**	error
b	in other	**2**	experience
c	learning by	**3**	future
d	life and	**4**	less
e	more or	**5**	life
f	past and	**6**	social
g	professional and	**7**	up
h	right and	**8**	words
i	so to sum	**9**	work
j	trial and	**10**	world
k	all over the	**11**	wrong
l	the rest of his	**12**	effect

C Students often use abbreviations in lecture notes.

  1 Read the student notes below from a lecture on Piaget. What did the lecturer say?

  2 Read Skills Check 2 and check your ideas.

9/8/1896	b. Sw.
'14	U. of Neuchâtel
'18	PhD
'19	→ Fr. – lecturer
'21	returned Sw.
3 yrs later	m., = 3 ch.
next 40 yrs	jobs @ uni, research inst.
16/9/1980	d. (Geneva)

D Sometimes lectures contain stories or ideas.

  1 Read Skills Check 3.

  2 There are two stories in the Piaget lecture. What are they? Write some notes to help you remember the story later.

Skills Check 1

Fixed phrases

Words often occur together in two-, three-, four- or even five-word phrases. It is easier to understand spoken language if you recognise complete phrases, rather than just single words. There are a number of fixed phrases in the lecture in Lesson 2.

Examples: *trial and error, more or less*

Skills Check 2

Using abbreviations in notes

You can take notes from lectures in your own language or in English. If you take notes in English, it is important to use abbreviations. However, you must be able to understand the abbreviations later, so it is best to use standard abbreviations. Here are some common ones.

1 Life events:

    m. = married

    b. = born

    d. = died

    ch. = children

    yr(s) = years

2 Dates: D/M/Y, e.g., 9/8/96 = 9th August, 1896

3 Years: apostrophe + last two numbers, e.g., '21 = 1921

4 Places: Capital letter + one more letter, e.g., Sw = Switzerland

5 People: Capital letter for a name that appears often, e.g., P. = Piaget.

Note the full stop in many abbreviations.

Skills Check 3

Taking notes of stories, ideas, etc.

Don't try to take detailed notes of stories, ideas, etc.

1 Listen for the start of the story. You will hear something like:

  • *There is an interesting story about …*

  • *One of Piaget's theories is …*

  • *I'd like to tell you about one case …*

2 Try to understand the gist (or idea) of the story.

3 Write a few words to remind yourself later. If you *understand* the story or idea *during* the lecture, you will *remember* it later.

Lesson 4: Applying new skills

A These multi-syllable words are all in the lecture (Lesson 2).
1 Mark the stress in each word.
2 🔊 Listen and check your ideas.

a career
b research
c explanation
d knowledge
e infancy
f adulthood
g professional
h social
i experience
j effect
k algebra
l react
m error
n trial
o theory

B 🔊 You are going to hear the second lecture about child development. Listen to the introduction. Make a set of outline notes.

C 🔊 Listen to the first part of the lecture.
1 Make notes on the main events in Erikson's life. Use standard abbreviations (see Skills Check 2, page 13).
2 There is one story in this part. One student wrote *Prince of Denmark*. Why?

D 🔊 Listen to the second part of the lecture.
1 What was Erikson's first book called?
2 What was Erikson's theory about?
3 What are you going to call the stories in this part?

E 🔊 Listen to the third part of the lecture. Complete the table of Erikson's stages of development.

Table 1: Erikson's stages of child development

stage	age range	good result	bad result
1	*birth–1/2 yrs.*	*trust*	*mistrust*
2			
3			
4			
5			

F 🔊 These statements are true or probably true. Listen to the lecture again and find evidence.
1 We don't know the name of Erik's real father.
2 We don't know when Erik left school.
3 He got married in Austria.
4 Erikson is a Danish family name.
5 His wife's name was Joan.
6 Erikson had problems with his own identity.
7 Children enter and leave the stages at different ages.
8 *Shame* is the noun from the adjective *ashamed*.
9 Children like dressing up as adults in Erikson's third stage.
10 Children enjoy games like football in Erikson's fourth stage.

G Compare the table of Piaget's stages and the table of Erikson's stages. Find some differences and some similarities.

In this theme you are going to hear two lectures on motivation at work.

Lesson 1: Vocabulary

You are going to learn some of the vocabulary you will need to understand the lectures.

A The red words are missing from this text.

1 Complete the text with one of the red words in each space. Make any necessary changes. You can use the same word more than once.

2 Write a price in dollars in the final space.

3 🔘 Listen and check your answers.

We often use _____ in business. For example, the price of something in a shop usually _____ the cost to make it plus some profit for the company. We can write this as an _____: cost + profit = price. Both _____ of an equation must be the same. In other words, they must _____. So if the cost is $20 and the profit is $2, the price must be $22. What happens if the cost _____? We can use our _____ to make sure the profit stays the same. If the _____ cost was $20 and the _____ cost is $22, then the new price must be _____.

B Here are some more equations from business. This time, the green words and phrases are missing.

1 Complete the equations with one of the green words in each space. Make any necessary changes. You can use the same word more than once.

2 Complete the example equation in each case.

3 🔘 Listen and check your answers.

Equation 1: salary per hour × _____ per week = total salary per week
Example: $10 × 48 hours = _____

Equation 2: working hours per day – _____ = total working hours per day
Example: 8 hours – 1.5 hours = _____

Equation 3: managers + workers = _____
Example: 5 managers + 100 workers = _____

C In the lectures in this theme, you are going to hear:
  • some new words that come from words you know already ('old' words).
  • some old words used in new ways.

1 Read the old word in each case (a–e, below).

2 🔘 Listen to each sentence. What form of the word do you hear? What does the word mean in this situation?

a product _____   **d** team _____

b product _____   **e** need _____

c industry _____

D Find the multi-syllable red and green words.

1 Mark the stressed syllable in each case.

2 🔘 Listen and check your ideas.

---

balance *(v)*

current *(adj)*

equal *(v)*

equation *(n)*

increase *(v)*

previous *(adj)*

side *(n)*

employee *(n)*

industrial *(adj)*

need *(n)*

produce *(v)*

production *(n)*

rest break *(n)*

team *(n)*

working hours *(n)*

Lesson 2: Listening

A Which of these aspects of a job are most important for you?
Give each aspect a number 1–3 (1 = very important, 2 = important, 3 = not important).
___ Good salary
___ Good relationships with the managers
___ Good relationships with colleagues
___ Interesting work
___ Good working conditions – rest breaks, working hours, etc.
___ Long-term security in the job – a 'job for life'
___ Recognition for good work

B You are going to hear two lectures from the Psychology course at Greenhill College. Read the information from the Psychology Faculty. What do you expect to find out …
1 in this week's lecture?
2 in next week's lecture?

C 🎧 Listen to the introduction. How does the lecturer define:
1 industrial psychology?
2 productivity?

D For the rest of this lesson, you are going to hear about Elton Mayo's life, work and ideas.
1 Read the Skills Check Reminder.
2 🎧 Listen to the first part of the lecture. Follow the suggestions in the Skills Check Reminder.

E 🎧 Listen to the second part of the lecture, which gives details of the experiment.
1 What did Mayo do? What happened on each occasion?
2 What conclusion did Mayo reach?

F 🎧 Listen to the third part. Each time the lecturer stops, answer her question.

G 🎧 Listen to the fourth part. What is the Hawthorne Effect?

H Show your notes to your partner. Can he/she understand them? Does it matter?

Greenhill College

Psychology Faculty   Semester 3

Week 1: *Introduction to Industrial Psychology*
• The life and work of Elton Mayo
• The Hawthorne Effect
• Explanation of the Hawthorne Effect

Week 2: *Motivation at Work*
• What is motivation?
• The life and work of Abraham Maslow
• Maslow's Hierarchy of Needs
• The life and work of Frederick Herzberg
• Herzberg's Hygiene Factors and Motivators

Skills Check

Reminder

In Theme 2 Lesson 2, you had to make notes about *either* the life events of a person *or* his work and ideas. In a real lecture, you have to make notes about **both things at the same time**.
You also learnt about making notes of stories. You learnt that you don't need to write full notes, just a few words to remind you of the story.

Suggestions:
1 Make notes about a person's *life* on the left-hand page of your notebook.
2 Make notes about his/her *ideas and work* on the right-hand page.
3 Write a few words to remind you of stories in a ⸻cloud⸻ and join the cloud to the relevant life event or idea.

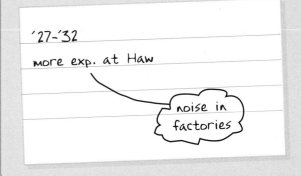

Lesson 3: Learning new skills

A We have seen that there are many fixed phrases in English. If you recognise a fixed phrase quickly, you can concentrate on the next part of the sentence.

   1 Complete each fixed phrase from the lecture in Lesson 2 with a preposition, e.g., *with*. You can use the same word more than once.

   2 📼 Listen and check your ideas.

B In Lesson 2 you heard information about the Hawthorne experiment. With an experiment, there will always be:

   1 The hypothesis: what the researcher thinks is true
   2 The experiment: what the researcher did
   3 The findings: what happened
   4 The conclusion: what the researcher decided about the findings

Summarise the main information in the lecture under these headings.

C We saw in the previous theme that students often use abbreviations in lecture notes.

   1 Read the student notes below from a lecture on Mayo. What did the lecturer say?

   2 Read Skills Check 1 and check your ideas.

```
26/12/80   b. Au.
'01          → UK
'23          → USA
              teach @ U. of Penn.
              → prof. @ Ha. Bus. Sch.
'24-'27     exp. @ Haw.
              light = ↑prod.?
              = no change
```

D The lecturer in Lesson 2 talked about noise in factories.

   1 What did she say?
   2 Why did she say this?
   3 How did she start and finish this part?
   4 Read Skills Check 2.
   5 📼 Listen to this part of the lecture again.

---

it all started __with__
_____ this day
_____ fact
_____ the circumstances
_____ other words
getting back _____ the point
_____ average
_____ total
_____ work
_____ example
_____ put it another way

Skills Check 1

Using signs in notes

We can often use signs instead of words. Here are some common ones:

+	and
=	is
>	more than
<	less than
↑	go / went up
↓	go / went down
→	move / change to / then / later
@	at
?	perhaps / is it true?

Skills Check 2

Recognising digressions

Lecturers sometimes **digress** from the subject. In other words, they start to talk about something else. You must recognise the start and finish of digressions.

start	*I remember once …* *I don't know if you know /* *have seen / have ever been …* *It's like my mother / father …*
finish	*Anyway …* *Getting back to the point …* *That's not really important.* *Where was I? Oh, yes.*

Be careful: digressions *sometimes* make a point that you should remember.

Lesson 4: Applying new skills

A The lecturer has given the students in the Psychology Faculty a personality quiz. Follow the instructions.

B 🔊 Listen to the introduction. How does the lecturer define:
1 industrial psychology?
2 the Hawthorne Effect?
3 motivation?

C What is the digression in this part of the lecture? Is there a point that you should remember from the digression? If so, what is it?

D 🔊 Listen to the first part of the lecture. Make notes on the life of Maslow.

E The lecturer is going to talk about Maslow's Hierarchy of Needs.
1 Look at Figure 1. What do you think a *hierarchy* is?
2 Which words in the diagram are new to you? Can you guess what any of them mean?
3 Why are the needs written as a triangle or pyramid?

F 🔊 Listen to the second part of the lecture. Check your answers to Exercise E.

G 🔊 Listen to the third part of the lecture. Make notes on the life of Herzberg.

H Herzberg's theory developed the work of Maslow.
1 🔊 Look at Figure 1 again. Listen to the fourth part. Label each item in the figure either *Hygiene factor* (H) or *Motivator* (M).
2 Define Herzberg's two factors.

I 🔊 Listen to the fifth part.
1 What does Herzberg's theory mean for managers?
2 What notes did you make of the story?

J Look back at your answers to the personality quiz in Exercise A. Read the interpretation. Do you agree that these are your needs?

Greenhill College

Psychology Faculty

What do you need from your life and your work?

Do the personality quiz and find out.

DO NOT SHOW YOUR ANSWERS OR DISCUSS THEM WITH ANYONE.

Read the following sets of statements. Tick any that apply to you. There are no right or wrong answers. You will get the interpretation after Lecture 2.

A I know that I am successful in my life and college work. My colleagues recognise that I am successful, too.

B I am part of a loving family. I have good relationships with my friends and colleagues – they accept me for who I am.

C I get bored easily. I constantly need to do new things, to challenge myself.

D I feel safe and secure at home and at college. My life generally has routine and structure.

E I have never really been hungry and I have always had a safe place to live. I don't really think about getting food or drink or a 'roof over my head'.

Figure 1: Maslow's Hierarchy of Needs

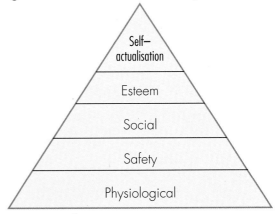

Interpretation:
Which statements did you *not* tick? You have those needs. See the explanation below.

I didn't tick ...	... so I have ...
C	Self-actualisation needs
A	Esteem needs
B	Social needs
D	Safety needs
E	Physiological needs

In this theme you are going to hear two talks about violent winds.

Lesson 1: Vocabulary

You are going to learn some of the vocabulary you will need to understand the talks.

A Read the quiz questions about the Sahara Desert.
  1 Choose the best answer to each question.
  2 📼 Listen and check your answers.

	1	2	3
a How much of the African continent does the Sahara occupy?	¹/₄	¹/₃	¹/₂
b How much of the land surface of the Earth does the Sahara occupy?	around 8%	about 18%	> 80%
c How big is the Sahara?	about 8,000 km²	around 80,000 km²	c. 8,000,000 km²
d How fast is the Sahara expanding?	c. 1 km p.m.	> 10 km p.m.	< 1 km p.a.
e How many different types of plants are there in the Sahara?	c. 100	c. 1,000	10,000

B Read the information about the *haboob*.
  1 Find a suitable green word for each space.
  2 📼 Listen and check your ideas.
  3 Draw a diagram of the formation of the *haboob*.

C Test each other on the information about the *haboob* in pairs.

D Discuss these questions in groups.
  1 Have you ever seen a *haboob* or a smaller sandstorm?
  2 What happened?

Name	*haboob*
Definition	*turning sandstorm or dust storm*
_____ of name	*Ar. = 'strong wind'*
Size	*→ 2 km wide*
	→ 1km high
_____	*50 kph → 80 kph*
_____	*1 → 3 hrs*
Location	*Sahara;* *SW of US*
_____	*May → Sept.;* *aft. or eve.*
_____	*Air falls from thunderclouds in their final stage. When it hits the ground, it picks up huge amounts of sand or dust. The wall of sand moves forward with the thunderclouds.*

around / about (= approx) *(prep)*

desert *(n)*

expand *(n)*

occupy *(v)*

plant *(n)*

surface *(n)*

the Earth *(n)*

duration *(n)*

formation *(n)*

lightning *(n)*

occur *(v)*

origin *(n)*

reach (= max. amount) *(v)*

sandstorm *(n)*

speed *(n)*

thunder *(n)*

timing *(n)*

Lesson 2: Listening

Ⓐ Look at the photograph.

1 What can you see in the picture?

2 Have you ever seen one of these?

3 What about dust devils?

Ⓑ Read the information about a radio programme.

1 What is the series about?

2 What is this programme about?

3 Can you think of other topics for programmes in this series?

Ⓒ Make a list of questions that you expect this programme to answer.

Example:

What are tornadoes?

Where do they occur?

Ⓓ 📼 Listen to the first part of the talk.

1 Which questions in Exercise C is Roger Dawkins going to answer? Number them in order.

2 Write outline headings for your notes. Use words instead of questions.

Examples:

What are tornadoes? = *Definition*

Where do they occur? = *Location*

Ⓔ 📼 Listen to the second part of the talk. Make notes of *important* information under each heading. If you get lost, don't worry! Leave a space in your notes. Wait for Roger to start talking about the next point.

Ⓕ Did you leave any spaces in your notes?

1 Compare your notes with your partner.

2 What information is still missing from your notes?

Ⓖ Look at the illustrations. They show the three theories of tornado formation.

1 What does each illustration show?

2 📼 Listen to the third part of the talk. Label each illustration with the correct name.

3 Explain the three theories in pairs.

9.00–9.30 p.m.   *Violent nature*
In this series, Roger Dawkins, a scientist with the World Weather Bureau, talks about the violent side of weather.
This week: Tornadoes

Lesson 3: Learning new skills

A Many fixed phrases are pairs of words. Complete these pairs. The first three are from the talk in Lesson 2.

1 Summer or   *winter*
2 Daytime or   _____
3 Morning or   _____
4 Wind and   _____
5 Rain or   _____
6 Thunder and   _____
7 Cold and   _____
8 Warm and   _____

B Read Skills Check 1.
1 Memorise the phrases.
2 Test each other in pairs.

How can you introduce the topic?

Today I'm going to talk about …

C Find your notes from the talk in Lesson 2. What information is still missing? Ask your teacher for the information.

Example:
You: *How fast can tornadoes turn?*
T: *From 500 to 800 kilometres per hour.*

D Read these parts of the talk in Lesson 2.
1 What is the missing word / phrase in each case?
2 Read Skills Check 2.
3 Check your answers to D1 above.

a _____ don't confuse the turning speed with the travelling speed …

b _____ have seen that film of people trying to outrun a tornado …

c _____ most of them happen in just one part of the United States …

d _____ the duration of tornadoes covers a wide range …

e _____ we don't really know the exact cause of tornadoes …

f _____ where was I? Oh, yes, size and speed can vary …

E What is the most interesting / surprising thing you have learnt about tornadoes in this theme?

Skills Check 1

Signposts – reminder

Lecturers use **signpost language** to help you to understand the order of information.
Lecturers use signposts to:

introduce the topic	*Today I'm going to talk about …*
explain the structure of the lecture	*Firstly, I'm going to explain …* *Then, I'm going to describe …* *Finally, I'll give you …*
end a section	*So, we've seen that …*
begin a new section	*Now, let's consider …*
help listeners to organise notes	*There are three types of …* *Firstly / Secondly / Finally …*

If you get lost in a lecture, don't worry!
1 Leave a space in your notes.
2 Wait for the start of the next section.
3 Ask your colleagues for the missing information at the end of the lecture – or ask the lecturer if there is an opportunity at the end.

Skills Check 2

Mini-signposts

Major signposts tell you the organisation of the lecture / talk and of each section. **Mini-signposts** tell you something about the next piece of information – if you understand them.

Mini-signposts	I'm going to …
I don't know if you … *(saw / read / heard)*	tell a story / give an example
By the way, / *Incidentally,*	give an extra piece of information or a piece of advice
Similarly, / *Again,*	say something that is like a previous piece of information
In fact, / *Actually,*	give more detail about this information
Anyway,	go back to my previous subject
To sum up,	summarise the information from the previous section / the whole lecture

Lesson 4: Applying new skills

A These multi-syllable words are from the talk in Lesson 2.

tornado	electrical	seriously
kilometres	develop	destructive
violent	classify	vary
incidentally	damaged	effects

1 Mark the stress in each word.
2 What happens to the unstressed syllables in each case?
3  Listen and check your ideas.

B You are going to hear another talk about violent nature. What information do you expect to hear? In what order?

C Listen to the first part of the talk.
1 Check your ideas from Exercise B.
2 Make a set of outline notes.

D Listen to the second part of the talk. Make notes of the important points. Leave a space for any information that you miss.

E Work in pairs. Ask about the information that you missed.

F Use your notes to answer these questions.
1 What are the main differences between tornadoes and hurricanes?
2 What is the origin of the name *hurricane*?
3 What was the worst natural disaster in US history?
4 Why do the majority of hurricanes only happen in the tropics?
5 When do hurricanes happen in the North Indian Ocean?
6 What is the relationship between a Level 1 and a Level 5 hurricane?

G Listen to the talk again. Check your answers to the questions in Exercise F.

H Listen to the final part of the talk. Draw a diagram showing the formation of hurricanes according to each theory.

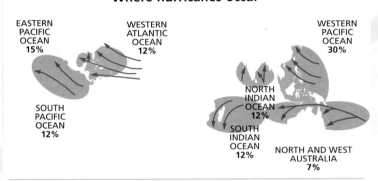

Where hurricanes occur

EASTERN PACIFIC OCEAN **15%**
WESTERN ATLANTIC OCEAN **12%**
WESTERN PACIFIC OCEAN **30%**
SOUTH PACIFIC OCEAN **12%**
NORTH INDIAN OCEAN **12%**
SOUTH INDIAN OCEAN **12%**
NORTH AND WEST AUSTRALIA **7%**

Table 1: The Saffir-Simpson Scale

scale	winds (kph)	damage
1	119–153	Minimal
2	154–177	Moderate
3	178–209	Extensive
4	210–249	Extreme
5	250+	Catastrophic

earthquake	volcano

agriculture *(n)*

climate *(n)*

difference *(n)*

different *(adj)*

industry *(n)*

population *(n)*

similarities *(n)*

temperature *(n)*

the economy *(n)*

the same *(adj)*

trading partner *(n)*

damage *(n and v)*

death *(n)*

erupt *(v)*

fire *(n)*

natural disaster *(n)*

rock *(n)*

shake *(v)*

tidal wave *(n)*

In this theme you are going to listen to two lectures about natural disasters.

Lesson 1: Vocabulary

You are going to learn some of the vocabulary you will need to understand the lectures.

A Make true sentences about your country. Use some of the red words.

B 🔊 Listen and look at the pictures. Copy the green words and phrases into one or both columns.

C Look at the pictures. Explain in your own words.
   1 What happens when there is an earthquake?
   2 What happens when a volcano erupts?

D Discuss the questions.
   1 Do you live in an earthquake area – or close to one?
   2 Have you ever experienced an earthquake? What happened?
   3 Do you live near a volcano? Which one?
   4 Have you ever seen a volcanic eruption?
   5 Have you ever experienced any other natural disaster? What happened?

Lesson 2: Listening

(A) You are going to hear a lecture about natural disasters.

🔊 Listen to the introduction. What exactly are you going to hear about in this lecture?

1 Tick one or more of the points in the green box.

2 Number the points in the order that you will hear about them.

3 Make an outline for notes on the lecture.

(B) Discuss these questions.

1 What were some early theories about earthquakes?

2 What is the real cause of earthquakes?

(C) 🔊 Listen to the first part of the lecture.

1 What were some of the early theories about the cause of earthquakes?

2 What was Aristotle's theory?

3 What is *seismology*? How did it get the name?

(D) 🔊 Listen to the second part of the lecture.

1 Take notes.

2 Ask about any important information that you missed.

(E) What do you expect to hear in the next part of the lecture?

1 Tick one or more of the following:
- information about different earthquakes around the world ___
- ways of measuring earthquakes ___
- information about famous seismologists ___
- the real cause of earthquakes ___

2 🔊 Listen to the third part and check your ideas.

(F) Look at the two world maps. What is the relationship between them?

1 Discuss.

2 🔊 Listen to the fourth part and check your ideas.

(G) What is the real cause of earthquakes?

🔊 Listen to the fifth part and draw a diagram from the information.

- a famous earthquake ___
- a famous volcanic eruption ___
- early theories about earthquakes ___
- early theories about volcanoes ___
- the real cause of earthquakes ___
- the real cause of volcanoes ___

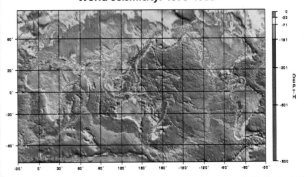

World seismicity: 1975-1995

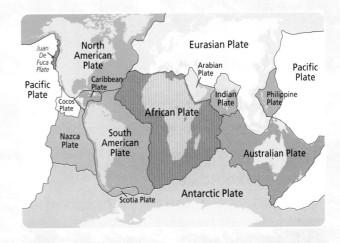

Lesson 3: Learning new skills

A There are many verbs about thinking.

1 Write each verb in the box in the correct row of the blue table.

believe	conclude	decide	propose
realise	say	suspect	think

This is true. I have evidence.	
This is true, but I have no evidence.	
This *might* be true. There is *some* evidence.	

2 Complete each sentence from the lecture in Lesson 2.

  a Some people thought _____, others believed _____. Some even said _____.

  b Aristotle thought _____.

  c After the Lisbon earthquake, scientists in Europe realised _____.

  d In the early 19th century, scientists suspected _____.

  e Gilbert decided _____.

  f Reid concluded _____.

  g Wegener proposed _____.

3 🔊 Listen and check your ideas.

B There are a lot of questions in the lecture in Lesson 2.

1 Complete these questions.
  Do earthquakes _____?
  Do volcanoes _____?
  What is the relationship between _____?
  What is a fault line? How _____?
  How do the plates _____?

2 Why does the lecturer ask the questions?

3 Read Skills Check 1 and check your ideas.

C Read Skills Check 2.

1 🔊 Listen to the first signposts from the lecture in Lesson 2. Can you remember how the lecturer continues in each case?

2 🔊 Listen and check your ideas.

3 🔊 Listen to some more first signposts. What will come next?

Skills Check 1

Rhetorical questions

Lecturers often ask questions during a lecture. In many cases, they do not want **you** to answer. **They** are going to answer the question in the next or later part of the lecture. These questions are called **rhetorical**.

Examples:

Do earthquakes cause volcanoes?
Do volcanoes cause earthquakes?
Or does something else cause both of them?
This week we are going to look at earthquakes, next week we will look at volcanoes …

When a lecturer asks a question during a lecture:

1 make a note, e.g., *quakes* ➜ *volcs?*

2 wait to see if the lecturer is going to continue; do not put your hand up or start to answer the question.

Skills Check 2

Two-sided signposts

We know that lecturers use a lot of signposts and mini-signposts to prepare the listener.

Examples:

Signpost	***This week we are going to hear about*** *early theories of the cause of earthquakes…*
Mini-signpost	***In fact****, the Greek word for shaking is* seismos

Lecturers also use **two-sided signposts**. The first part prepares you for the second part.

Examples:

First signpost	Second signpost
On the one hand*,*	***On the other*** (hand),
One *(does something)*	***The other*** *(does something different)*
Some people *(do / think something)*	***Other people*** *(do / think something different)*
… not … *(this thing / idea)*	***Instead****,* *(a different thing / idea)*
At first*,* *(this idea)*	***but then / gradually*** *(a different idea)*

Lesson 4: Applying new skills

A These multi-syllable words are from the lecture in Lesson 2.

natural	communications
disaster	geology
explodes	eventually
earthquake	evidence
volcano	concluded
observations	meteorologist

1 Mark the stress in each word.
2 What happens to the unstressed syllables in each case?
3 🎧 Listen and check your ideas.

B You are going to listen to the next lecture about natural disasters. What is the lecturer going to talk about? Make a list of points in order.

C 🎧 Listen to the introduction.
1 Check your ideas from Exercise B.
2 Make a set of outline notes.

D 🎧 Listen to the first part of the lecture.
1 Make notes of the important points.
2 Complete these sentences:
   a *Some people believed …*
   b *Others thought …*
   c *Aristotle said …*

E What is the lecturer going to talk about next?
1 Check your outline notes.
2 Can you guess any of the information to complete Table 1?
3 🎧 Listen to the second part and check or complete the table.
4 What was special about the archaeologist's excavations?

F 🎧 Listen to the third part of the lecture. Draw a diagram to show the modern theory of volcano formation.

G 🎧 Listen to the fourth part of the lecture. Make notes of the important information.

H How is the lecturer going to sum up?
1 Think of a possible conclusion.
2 🎧 Listen and check your ideas.

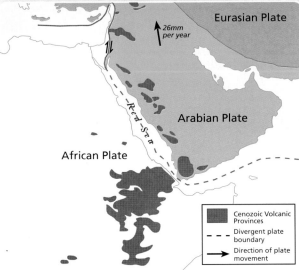

Table 1: The most famous volcanic eruption

Country	
Date	
Place	
Volcano	
Eyewitness	
Deaths	
Excavated in	
Archaeologist	

Figure 1: Plaster figure from Pompeii

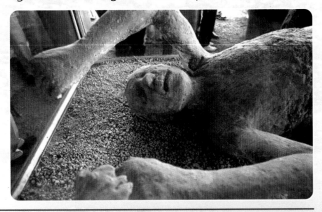

In this theme you are going to listen to lectures about society and the common features of cultures.

Lesson 1: Vocabulary

You are going to learn some vocabulary you will need to understand the lectures.

Ⓐ Discuss these questions. They use some of the red words.

1 What special *customs* do you have in your country to celebrate the *birth* of a child?
2 Are there any special *customs* in your country when someone comes of age?
3 How do you celebrate a *marriage* in your country?
4 What do you do in your country when someone dies?

Ⓑ 📼 Read and listen to this introduction to a lecture. Then complete the text with one of the green words in each space.

We talk a lot nowadays about society and culture and civilization. We even have a new branch of education – _____ – which is the study of society. But have you ever stopped to ask yourself: What is society? What is culture? What is civilization? What is the _____ between the three words? According to the dictionary, society is the organisation of _____ into social groups. Culture, on the other hand, is defined as the customs and _____ of a society. Individuals organise into social groups that become a _____. The society then develops customs and _____ certain things. This makes the society into a _____. What about a civilization? Again, the dictionary helps. A _____ is a culture that has achieved important _____ in science and art.

Ⓒ Study the words in the box.

1 Put the words in order, according to the information in the lecture.
2 Cover the text and explain your order to a partner.

civilization culture group individual society

Ⓓ Study the green words.

1 Mark the stressed syllables in the green words.
2 📼 Listen to these stressed syllables. Number the green words in the order you hear the stressed syllables.

birth (*n*)

customs (*n*)

get married (*v*)

marriage (*n*)

marry (*v*)

wedding (*n*)

achieve (*v*)

achievement (*n*)

advance (*n*)

culture (*n*)

individual (*n*)

relationship (*n*)

social (*adj*)

society (*n*)

sociology (*n*)

Lesson 2: Listening

A You are going to hear a lecture from the Sociology Faculty at Greenhill College.

1 Look at the handout. What are the missing words?

2 🎧 Listen to the introduction. Make notes. Check your answers to Exercise 1.

3 Make an outline for notes on the lecture.

B 🎧 Listen to the first part of the lecture.

1 When the lecturer pauses, complete the phrase or sentence. Listen and check your ideas.

2 How many questions from the handout has the lecturer answered in this part?

3 Make notes of the information.

C Look at the fifth question on the handout.

1 Discuss the question.

2 Read the Skills Check Reminder.

3 🎧 Listen to the second part of the lecture. Make notes.

D Complete the part of the lecture in the blue box with a word from the purple box in each space.

civilization	cohesion	force	groups
place	reason	religion	society	tribes

E Look at the sixth question on the handout.

1 Discuss the question. Make a list.
   e.g., *All cultures have their own laws.*

2 Compare your list with the features in the green box.

3 🎧 Listen to the third part of the lecture. Number the features in the green box in order.

F Summarise the point the lecturer makes about each feature. Try to remember the example, if there is one.

Greenhill College

Faculty: Sociology   Semester 3

Topic: Society, culture and civilization (1)

In this week's lecture, we try to answer some of the basic questions in sociology:

1 What is _____?

2 What is a _____?

3 What is a _____?

4 What is the _____ between society, culture and civilization?

5 Is it natural for people to form into social _____? (Ibn Khaldoun)

6 What are the common _____ of a society or culture?

Skills Check

Reminder

When you take notes about a person:

- use **abbreviations** and **signs**.
- put notes about the person's **life** on the **left**-hand page or side of your notebook.
- put notes about the person's **ideas** and **work** on the **right**-hand page or side.
- recognise **digressions**.

Ibn Khaldoun believed in the idea of 'asabiyah, which can be translated as 'social _____', or joining together. He said that this cohesion appears naturally in _____ and other small social _____. He went on to claim that the social cohesion will be stronger if the society develops a strong _____. Ibn Khaldoun thought that social cohesion was the driving _____ of society, the thing that pushes the _____ forwards and makes it strong. When the cohesion weakens, for any _____, the society weakens and another _____ with a stronger cohesion takes its _____.

---

education	food and cooking	language
laws	leisure	rites of passage	social norms
stories	technology	trade

Lesson 3: Learning new skills

A Read these sentences from the lecture (Lesson 2).
  1 Think of a suitable word or words to complete each fixed phrase.
  2 🔊 Listen and check your ideas.

    a _____ the dictionary, society is the organisation of individuals into groups.
    b Culture, on the other hand, is _____ the customs and achievements of a society.
    c Incidentally, the Khalduniyah area in Tunis has hardly changed since _____.
    d The death of his parents had a deep effect on Ibn Khaldoun, as _____.
    e That's about a third of the population at the time. Imagine _____. 1 in 3 people died.
    f The form of education _____ the society.
    g People have time for leisure. In _____, they are not working every _____ of the _____.
    h English people call French people 'frogs' because some French people eat frogs' legs. In _____, French people used to call English people *le rote boeuf,* or the roast beef, because they ate roast beef.
    i The _____ that traditional food and methods of cooking are very important to a cultural group.

B Read these sentences from the lecture.
  1 What is the important difference between Sentences A and B?

A	B
Ibn Khaldoun was born in Tunis in 1332.	Social cohesion appears naturally in small social groups.
Ibn Khaldoun's father was an important man.	Social cohesion will be stronger if the society develops a strong religion.
When Ibn Khaldoun was only 16, the Black Death killed both his parents.	Social cohesion is the driving force of society. When the cohesion weakens, for any reason, the society weakens.

  2 Read Skills Check 1. Check your answers.
  3 🔊 Listen to a section of the lecture again. How does the lecturer show that Sentences B are Ibn Khaldoun's opinion?

C Read these words from the lecture.
  … the death of his parents from the Black Death had a deep effect on Ibn Khaldoun.
  1 Is this a fact or an opinion?
  2 If it is an opinion, whose opinion? Ibn Khaldoun's or the lecturer's?
  3 Read Skills Check 2 then explain your answer.

D Work in groups.
  🔊 Listen again to the last part of the lecture in Lesson 2. After each section, give an example from your own culture.

Skills Check 1

Distinguishing fact from opinion

Lecturers often give:
- **facts** about a famous person.
- the famous **person's opinions**.

It is usually quite easy to distinguish between facts and opinions.

Examples:

Facts	Opinions
Ibn Khaldoun was born in Tunis in 1332.	He thought that social cohesion is the driving force of society.

Listen for **introductory verbs**:
*He / she **thought** / **claimed** / **said** / **believed** …*
But be careful. Sometimes lecturers do not use an introductory verb.

Example:
When the cohesion weakens, for any reason, the society weakens. = opinion

---

Skills Check 2

Whose opinion?

Lecturers sometimes give their **own opinion** about information in the lecture.
You must identify the lecturer's own opinions.

Example:

Introduction	Opinion
I believe / I'm sure / No doubt / Obviously	the death of his parents from the Black Death had a deep effect on Ibn Khaldoun.

Lesson 4: Applying new skills

A Match the adjectives and nouns. They are all used in the lecture in Lesson 2.

1	common	disease
2	certain	effect
3	terrible	features
4	deep	food
5	massive	force
6	driving	group
7	social	introduction
8	strong	religion
9	primitive	society
10	traditional	things

B You are going to hear another lecture from the Sociology Faculty at Greenhill College.
  1 Look at the handout. What could the missing words be?
  2 📼 Listen to the introduction and check your answers.
  3 Make an outline for notes on the lecture.

C Look at the first question on the handout.
  1 Discuss the question.
  2 📼 Listen to the first part of the lecture. For each of the four people mentioned, put either S > I or I > S.
  3 📼 Listen again and complete the summary in the blue box.

D Look at the second question on the handout.
  1 Discuss the question.
  2 📼 Listen to the second part of the lecture. Make notes of Ibn Khaldoun's opinions.
  3 Complete the summary of his ideas in the green box.

E The lecturer gives some of his own opinions during this part.
  📼 Listen to the second part again and identify them.

F Look at the third question on the handout.
  1 Discuss the question.
  2 📼 Listen to the third part of the lecture. Complete the statements in the bubbles.

G Which writer do you agree with most? Hegel, De Caritat or Wells. Why?

Greenhill College

Faculty: Sociology   Semester 3

Topic: Society, culture and civilization (2)

In this week's lecture, we try to answer some more basic questions in sociology:

1 Is society more important than _____, or are _____ more important than society? (Aristotle, Sophocles, Durkheim, Weber)

2 Do all societies go through the same _____? (Ibn Khaldoun)

3 Do we learn from _____, or do we keep repeating the same _____? (Hegel, De Caritat, Wells)

Aristotle and Sophocles both believed that a person is only a real human being when he or she is _____ ____ _____. Durkheim said that individuals depend on _____ ____ _____ and that people have a deep need to _____ _____ _____. Weber thought that _____ _____ is more important than _____. He believed that the world only works when people act _____ _____.

Ibn Khaldoun thought that all societies go through three stages as follows:
They _____. They produce _____ in technology, in science and in _____. They _____ – because of internal or _____ influences.

The only thing we learn from history is that _____.

Hegel

One day individuals will be _____. We can learn from our _____. There is no limit to human _____.

De Caritat

Human history becomes more and more a race between _____ and _____.

H.G. Wells

In this theme you are going to listen to two talks about great advances in history.

Lesson 1: Vocabulary

You are going to learn some vocabulary you will need to understand the talks.

A The diagram in Figure 1 shows the circle of progress in the history of the world.

   1 📼 Listen and complete the diagram with a red word in each space.

   2 Give an example of the circle for a particular idea, e.g., *An inventor thinks 'Things move easily when they can roll on top of something.'*

Figure 1: The circle of progress

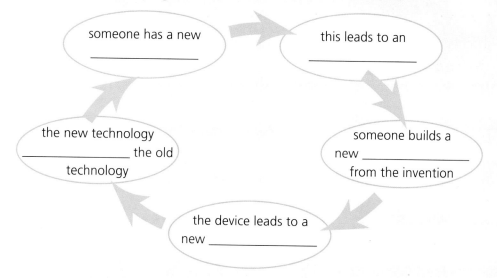

build (v)

device (n)

idea (n)

inventor (n)

replace (v)

technology (n)

antibiotics (n)

engine (n)

preservation (n)

printing (n)

wheel (n)

B 📼 Listen to some information about a radio programme.

   1 What programme is this about?

   2 What are 'advances', according to the presenter?

   3 What must be true about any advance?

   4 What does the presenter want you to do now?

   5 Where should you send the e-mail?

   6 How can you hear the results?

C Look at the shortlist of the greatest advances in history.

   1 Write a green word in each space.

   2 📼 Listen to the radio programme. Number the advances in order.

D Which of these eight advances would you put at number one? Why?

Table 1: The shortlist of great advances

_____	They prevent or cure diseases.
Food _____	It means that people don't have to go shopping every day.
Mass _____	It means that we can make products quickly and cheaply.
The computer	It has revolutionised office work, mathematics, communications … almost everything!
The internal combustion _____	It is the device that powers cars, lorries, some ships, some planes, etc.
The _____ press	It means we can print books quickly.
The telephone	It means we can talk to anyone anywhere.
The _____	It enables us to move heavy things with less effort.

8.50–9.00

The 10-Minute Debate

What is the most important advance that people have made in the history of the world?

Each week, we invite someone to tell us which invention or discovery is, in his or her opinion, the most important in the history of the world.
This week: Anne Robertson

Lesson 2: Listening

A Read the information about a radio programme. How would you answer the question?
   1 Make a list of the five most important advances in the history of the world. Use some from Lesson 1 if you want to.
   2 Number them in order of importance.

B 🔊 Listen to Anne's talk straight through.
   1 Tick any advances from your list in Exercise A.
   2 Which advance does Anne choose?
   3 Why does she dismiss the other alternatives?

C How does Anne support her argument?
   1 Which of the points in the blue box does she make? Tick one or more.
   2 🔊 Listen again and check your answers.

D All the ticked points in the blue box are Anne's personal opinions.
   1 Which ones do you agree with?
   2 Which do you think is her strongest point? Why?

E What do you think of Anne's choice? Explain your answer.

F What sort of foods can you preserve by …
   1 drying?
   2 salting?
   3 pickling?
   4 canning?
   5 freezing?

Advances in food preservation are more fundamental than advances in transport or communications.	
Ancient civilizations had no way of keeping food.	
Civilization develops in settled communities.	
Food preservation has given women more time to live.	
Food preservation was still a problem until quite recently.	
Food tastes better if you keep it for some time.	
If you have to gather food and go hunting every day, there is very little time left for anything else.	
It is hard for civilization to develop if you have to move from place to place following animals.	
People get lots of diseases from food that is not preserved properly.	
Some civilizations died out because they did not know how to preserve food.	
Without food preservation, people would never have developed transport and communications.	

Lesson 3: Learning new skills

Ⓐ The phrases on the right are from the talk in Lesson 2.

1 Complete each phrase with a preposition or adverb in each space.

2 📼 Listen and check your ideas.

Ⓑ There are nine sections from the talk in the yellow box. They are not in order.

1 What is the speaker doing in each section?
Example: *In Section a the speaker is giving her opinion.*

2 Read the Skills Check. Match each section (1–9) in the Skills Check to one of the points (a–i) below. Write the letter in the second column.

3 Cover the yellow box. How did Anne do each of the things in the Skills Check?

> **a** *I believe the greatest advance that human beings have made is in food preservation.*
>
> **b** *Before food preservation existed, people could not settle down in one place and develop as a civilization.*
>
> **c** *However, I do not believe the greatest advance in the history of the world has got anything to do with transport.*
>
> **d** *Is it something to do with transport?*
>
> **e** *Not true. Throughout history, Man has struggled with the problem of preserving food.*
>
> **f** *OK, I hear you say. It was important in the old days to find a way of preserving food. But that problem was solved thousands of years ago.*
>
> **g** *So, in conclusion. Food preservation first made it possible for a community as a whole to have time off from gathering, hunting and preparing food.*
>
> **h** *It is true that the wheel, for example, revolutionised transport …*
>
> **i** *What is the most important advance that people have made in the history of the world?*

Ⓒ Find the list you made in Lesson 2 Exercise A. Make a list of points:

1 in support of your #1 choice.

2 in support of choices #2 and #3.

> **a** something to do _____
> **b** in the field _____
> **c** _____ a very real sense
> **d** months _____ a time
> **e** _____ the old days
> **f** carry it _____ their heads
> **g** all _____ the world
> **h** day _____, day _____
> **i** _____ sunrise _____ sunset
> **j** _____ place _____ place
> **k** _____ this case
> **l** _____ one place
> **m** the essence _____
> **n** _____ turn

Skills Check

Understanding a speaker's argument

We have seen that speakers often give **opinions** in lectures. Sometimes these are the opinions of **famous people** and sometimes they are the **speaker's own** opinion. We must distinguish fact from opinion in the middle of a lecture.

But sometimes the whole point of a talk is to give the speaker's opinion. This happens when a speaker is **arguing for a particular point of view**. He or she wants you to accept the opinion. When speakers are **arguing a case** in English, they often use this structure:

1 introduce the topic		*i*
2 suggest alternative opinions		
3 make points in support of the alternative opinions		
4 dismiss the alternative opinions		
5 introduce the speaker's opinion		
6 make points in support of the opinion		
7 recognise objections to the opinion		
8 deal with objections to the opinion		
9 sum up		

Lesson 4: Applying new skills

A Anne uses several fixed phrases in her talk in Lesson 2.

   1 Complete this part of the talk with a suitable phrase in each space.

   2 🔊 Listen again and check your ideas.

OK, I hear _____. It was important in _____ to find a way of preserving food. But that problem was solved thousands of years ago. Not true. Throughout _____, Man has struggled with the problem of preserving food. As _____, some progress was made with drying, salting and pickling thousands of years ago. But as _____ people moved away from a settled community, there were still great problems. Sailors often got a painful and potentially fatal disease called scurvy because they did not eat fresh fruit for _____. Scurvy struck the sailors on Magellan's journey around the world in 1519, for _____. The same situation was repeated all _____. Napoleon lost more men to scurvy and starvation in the war against Russia than he did in all the battles put _____. In _____, the problem for Napoleon was _____ bad _____ the French government offered a reward of 12,000 francs to the person who could solve it. The result was canning. A man called Nicholas Appert tried for years to win the prize. At _____, he had no success, but _____ he solved the problem. Finally, he put food into airtight bottles in _____ preserve it. It worked. So by the 20th century, a lot of foodstuffs could be preserved, but fresh meat and dairy products were still a problem _____ the 1950s.

B You are going to hear another talk from the radio series. Before you listen, here are some phrases and sentences from the talk. Match each one to a function.

introduce the topic	As I see it, neither computers nor mass production make our lives better in the most important way.
suggest alternative opinions	Before people understood the need for clean water, decent housing and waste disposal, life for most people was short and full of pain.
make points in support of the alternative opinions	In my opinion, the greatest advance that human beings have made is in the conquest of infectious diseases.
dismiss the alternative opinions	Mass production has certainly enabled us to change the world out of all recognition.
introduce the speaker's opinion	Of course, you could argue that computers and mass production have made people's lives better.
make points in support of the opinion	Some might say it is mass production –
recognise objections to the opinion	What is the most important advance that people have made in the history of the world?
deal with objections to the opinion	What is the point of having a long life if it is endless, hard, boring work?

C 🔊 Listen to the whole talk. Check your answers to Exercise B.

D Discuss these questions.

   1 What, in the speaker's opinion, is the greatest advance of all time?

   2 What points does the speaker make in support of this opinion?

E Which speaker (Lesson 2 or Lesson 4) do you agree with? Or do you think the greatest advance is something else?

In this theme you are going to hear two radio programmes about famous works of literature in English.

Lesson 1: Vocabulary

You are going to learn some vocabulary that you will need to understand the radio programmes.

A 🔲 Listen to the past tense of the red words. Number the infinitives in order.

B Here is some information about a radio programme. Read the information and answer the questions.

1 How many writers is the programme about?
2 What is the most famous book by each writer?
3 Can you explain the title of this week's programme?

C 🔲 Listen to the introduction to the programme. Answer the questions.

1 What is Gulliver's first name?
2 Where does he travel to?
3 Why does the presenter mention *The Voyages of Sindbad the Sailor?*
4 Is *Gulliver's Travels* a children's story?
5 Why did Swift write the book?
6 What happens to Robinson Crusoe?
7 Who is the story based on?
8 Is *Robinson Crusoe* a children's book?
9 What do some critics say about the book?
10 What does the presenter believe?

D Read the sentences from the introduction in the blue box.

1 Write a green word in each space. Make any necessary changes.
2 🔲 Listen and check your answers.

8.30–9.00 p.m.
Writers and their works
This week: One-hit wonders
Amanda Craig talks about two writers who each produced one great work. Firstly, she discusses Jonathan Swift and his book, *Gulliver's Travels.* Then she talks about *Robinson Crusoe*, the adventure story by Daniel Defoe. We also hear extracts from the two books.

a In Swift's book, the _____, Lemuel Gulliver, travels to four different worlds.
b *Gulliver's Travels* may even be _____ the Sindbad stories.
c It is certainly true that millions of children have enjoyed the stories in simplified _____.
d But the _____, Jonathan Swift, did not write the book for children.
e He wrote the stories as a _____ of the politicians in England at the time.
f *Robinson Crusoe* is one of the most famous _____ stories in the English language.
g It is now a _____ story with children, but Defoe probably didn't write it as a children's book.
h Some _____ say the story is an _____ for the fight between good and evil.
i I personally believe that Crusoe's life _____ the advance of civilization.

begin *(v)*

belong *(v)*

buy *(v)*

disappear *(v)*

explore *(v)*

hear *(v)*

land *(v)*

let *(v)*

light *(v)*

need *(v)*

search *(v)*

see *(v)*

sell *(v)*

spend *(v)*

think *(v)*

trick *(v)*

adventure *(n)*

allegory *(n)*

author *(n)*

base (on) *(v)*

criticism *(n)*

critic *(n)*

hero *(n)*

popular *(adj)*

represent *(v)*

version *(n)*

Lesson 2: Listening

Ⓐ You are going to hear part of a radio programme about English literature. You heard the introduction in Lesson 1.

1 Who are you going to hear about first?

2 What information do you expect to hear about him?

3 📼 Listen to the first part of the programme. Make notes.

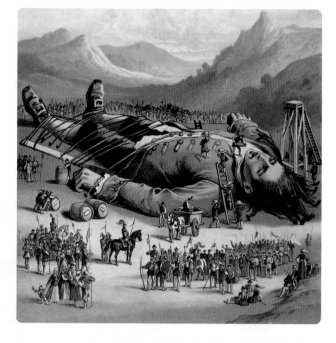

Ⓑ You are going to hear part of *Gulliver's Travels*.

1 Look at the picture. What happens in this part of the story?

2 📼 Listen to the first part. Number in order the events in the yellow box.

3 📼 Listen again and check your ideas.

4 What do you think happens next in the story?

Ⓒ 📼 Listen to the second part of the story. Complete these sentences with a word from the green box in each space.

countries	eggs	finger	country	world
day	end	future	law	years

1 The king's friend tells Gulliver about the problems in his

_____ .

2 He explains that there are two powerful _____ .

3 They have fought each other for many _____ .

4 The war is about _____ .

5 For many years, the people of Lilliput cut them at the big

_____ .

6 One day, the king's son cut his _____ while he was doing this.

7 So the king made a new _____ .

8 Everyone had to break their eggs at the little end in _____ .

9 People who disagreed with this law fled to the other _____ .

10 Now the other country is going to invade Lilliput any _____ .

- A lot of people climb onto Gulliver.
- Gulliver breaks some of the strings.
- Gulliver lifts his left hand.
- Gulliver shouts loudly.
- Gulliver tries to grab one of the people.
- Gulliver turns his head.
- Gulliver wakes up.
- Someone climbs onto Gulliver.
- The people fire arrows at Gulliver.
- The people jump off Gulliver.

Ⓓ What does Gulliver do?

1 Discuss in pairs.

2 📼 Listen to the third part of the story and check your ideas.

3 Do a cartoon version of this part of the story with pin men.

Ⓔ What does the story of Gulliver in the country of Lilliput teach us about the world?

1 Discuss in pairs.

2 📼 Listen to the final part and check your ideas.

Lesson 3: Learning new skills

A There are several proper nouns – names of people and places – in the story in Lesson 2.

1 🔘 Listen again to the proper nouns. Write the words. Guess the spelling.

2 Read Skills Check 1.

3 🔘 Listen again and check your spelling.

B Study these sentences from Lesson 2.

I felt something <u>creeping</u> up my arm.

<u>Peering</u> down, I saw a human creature …

1 Guess the meaning of each underlined word.

2 Read Skills Check 2 and check.

3 🔘 Listen to some sentences from the story. Match the dramatic verbs with the common verbs in the blue box.

4 Make a sentence about Gulliver with each of the dramatic verbs.

fled (flee)	catch
leap / plunge	jump
grab	move
creep	pull
haul / wrench / drag	run away
cry	shout

C Study these sentences from the story.

This is an <u>immense</u> distance for the little men …

The enemy was so <u>terrified</u> when they saw me …

1 Guess the meaning of each underlined word.

2 Read Skills Check 3 and check.

3 Match the extreme adjectives and the meanings in the green box.

4 Make a sentence about Gulliver with each of the extreme adjectives.

freezing	very hot
boiling	very hungry
exhausted	very wet
starving	very large
parched	very small
soaking	very thirsty / dry
enormous	very tired
tiny	very cold

Skills Check 1

Guessing the spelling of proper nouns

Speakers often do not spell proper nouns – the names of people and places. You have to guess the spelling, and check it later.

Consonants are easy, but remember some consonant sounds can be spelt in different ways, e.g., /f/ = f or *ph*.

Here are some common **vowel** patterns:

/æ/	= a	/ɑː/	a or ar
/e/	= e	/ɜː/	er
/ɪ/	= i	/iː/	ee
/ɒ/	= o	/ɔː/	or
/ʌ/	= u	/uː/	oo

You cannot guess the vowel when you hear the sound schwa (/ə/). Write any vowel and check later.

Skills Check 2

Understanding dramatic language (1)

Writers of fiction often use dramatic **verbs** for more common ones.

Examples: creeping

I felt something ~~moving~~ up my arm.

Peering

~~Looking~~ down, I saw a human creature …

Don't worry if the verb is not familiar to you. Just work out the meaning from the context. If you can remember the word, check its precise meaning later.

Examples:

creeping = moving very slowly

peering = looking very closely

Skills Check 3

Understanding dramatic language (2)

Writers of fiction often use extreme **adjectives** for more common ones.

Examples:

      an immense

This is ~~a very big~~ distance for the little men …

               terrified

The enemy was so ~~very frightened~~ when they saw me …

Don't worry if the adjective is not familiar to you. Just work out the meaning from the context.

Lesson 4: Applying new skills

A You are going to hear the second half of the radio programme about *one-hit wonders* in English literature.
  1 Who are you going to hear about this time?
  2 What information do you expect to hear about him?
  3 📼 Listen to the first part of the programme. Make notes.

B You are going to hear part of *Robinson Crusoe*.
  1 Look at the picture. What happens in this part of the story?
  2 What should Crusoe try to find on the ship? Tick five items in the yellow box. Explain your choices.
  3 📼 Listen to the first part of the story. Number the items in the yellow box in the order that Crusoe finds them.
  4 What do you think happens next in the story?

C 📼 Listen to the second part of the story.
  1 What do you find out about Crusoe's location? Make notes.
  2 Do a cartoon version of this part of the story with Crusoe as a pin man.

D What is *Robinson Crusoe* about?
  1 Discuss in pairs.
  2 📼 Listen to the final part of the programme. What do some critics think the book is about? What about the presenter? Make notes.
  3 📼 Listen again. When the presenter pauses, predict the next word. Then listen and check.

Robinson Crusoe, saving his Goods out of the Wreck of his Ship.

biscuits	knives
books	meat
bread	money
cheese	paper
clothes	pens
corn	rice
guns	swords
ammunition	tools

What is *Robinson Crusoe* about? At one _____, it is just an _____ story, and a very good one at that. But some _____ have found a lot more in the book. Some say it is a rites of _____ book with one man struggling to survive and, in the _____, growing up. Others say there is more to it than _____. At the beginning of the story, Crusoe is not a very nice _____. Each time he sets _____, he is shipwrecked. Some say this is _____ for his _____. Finally, he arrives on his desert _____. He builds a home and grows _____ and raises _____. He eventually finds a _____ on the island and teaches him to believe in _____. Finally, he wins several battles against _____ who try to invade from nearby _____. I believe that *Robinson Crusoe* is the story of _____ told through the eyes of one _____.

In this theme you are going to listen to a lecture about tourism.

Lesson 1: Vocabulary

You are going to learn some vocabulary that you will need to understand the lecture.

A 🔲 Listen to a text about sport. Number the red words in the order you hear them.

B 🔲 Listen to a short text that contains the green words. Then complete the text with one of the words in each space. Make any necessary changes.

_____ is big business nowadays. The _____ in travel for leisure has been enormous in the last half century, especially the increase in _____ holiday travel. For example, most people in Western Europe have now visited at least one other country, whereas 50 years ago only a tiny percentage of Europeans had been _____.

There are _____ to holiday travel on this massive scale. On the _____ side, people learn about other cultures when they travel. Perhaps it is harder to go to war against a country that you have visited on holiday. On the _____ side, tourism often has a big _____ on the holiday destinations. _____ sometimes destroy the things they have come to see. For example, visitors to the tombs in Egypt have damaged the old wall paintings with the flashlights of their cameras. _____ sometimes turn parts of the foreign country into little versions of their own country. For instance, English _____ to Spain has led to Spanish shops and restaurants selling English food rather than Spanish.

Why do people travel hundreds or even thousands of miles on holiday? Clearly, some want sun and sand, others want to see the ruins of an ancient civilization or just experience the _____ of a different culture. A lot of tourism is _____ – simply going to look at buildings or landscapes in a different country. Personally, I think most _____ just want to tell their friends later, 'I've been there, I've seen that and I've got the photographs'.

C Discuss these questions.

1 What are the pros and cons of international tourism, according to the speaker in Exercise B?
2 Why do most tourists go abroad, according to the speaker in Exercise B?
3 In what ways do other cultures have different lifestyles?
4 What would be your ideal holiday destination – *sun, sand, ruins ...*?

---

athlete *(n)*

compete *(v)*

event *(n)*

fit *(adj)*

physical fitness *(n)*

practice *(n)*

practise *(v)*

race *(n)*

sportsman *(n)*

sportswoman *(n)*

throw *(v)*

train *(v)*

abroad *(adj)*

growth *(n)*

impact *(n)*

international *(adj)*

lifestyle *(n)*

negative *(adj)*

positive *(adj)*

pros and cons *(n)*

sightseeing *(n)*

tourism *(n)*

tourist *(n)*

Lesson 2: Listening

A Think about tourism in your country.
1 What percentage of national income does it account for? Guess.
2 Why do tourists come to your country? Make a list of reasons.
3 Number the reasons in order of importance.
4 What might *stop* tourists coming to your country?

B You are going to hear a lecture from a faculty at Greenhill College.
1 Read the handout. What is the faculty and the course?
2 How would you answer the question on the handout?
3 ▣ Listen to the introduction. How does the lecturer answer the question?

C A student made an outline set of notes from the introduction to the lecture.
1 Read and correct her outline.
2 ▣ Listen to the introduction again and check your ideas.

D How would you define 'tourism'?
1 Write a definition in one sentence.
2 ▣ Listen to the first part of the lecture. Is the lecturer's definition similar to yours?

E ▣ Listen to the second part of the lecture.
1 Make notes.
2 Why does the lecturer mention each of the things in the yellow box?

F The lecturer gave out two graphs at the beginning of this lecture (bottom right of page 41).
1 Study each graph. What does it show?
2 What is the missing information?
3 ▣ Listen to the third part of the lecture. Try to contribute to each discussion.
4 Look at the figures in the blue box. Why does the lecturer mention each figure?
▣ Listen to the third part of the lecture again and check your answers.

G What does the lecturer ask you to do at the end of this part? Follow his instructions.

Greenhill College

Faculty: *Sports and Leisure Management*
Course: *Tourism Management*

Lecture 1:
Introduction to the course

Why should you study Tourism Management?

Tourism Management

1. Size of tourism now

2. Impact of tourism
   2.1. bad effects
   2.2. good effects
3. Definition of tourism
4. History of tourism

NICE

- holy days
- the Grand Tour
- the railways
- seaside towns
- Thomas Cook

$5 trillion	7.6%
c $10 trillion	2.9%
c $30 trillion	nearly 4%
16%	5.5%
4%	just over 6%
3%	7%
195 m	2.8%

Lesson 3: Learning new skills

A The words in the yellow box make phrases. They are all from the lecture in Lesson 2.

1 Match the beginning and ending of each phrase.

2 🔊 Listen and check your ideas.

● Let me say	another way
● It is important	people
● It is only	recently that
● For thousands of	straight away
● The majority of	to say that
● It is fair	to understand
● We can look at this	years

B What do you expect to come after each of the phrases in the blue box?

1 Complete each sentence with something suitable.

2 🔊 Listen and check your ideas.

> ● Before we look at tourism as a business, …
> ● Tourism has a good effect in many cases, …
> ● … transport links were so bad that …
> ● According to …
> ● In terms of …
> ● Tourism is travel for pleasure. In other words, …

C You have made a list of positive and negative impacts of tourism.

1 🔊 Listen to the next part of the lecture. Tick the points the lecturer mentions.

2 Read the Skills Check.

3 🔊 Listen to this part of the lecture again. Make notes of the extra points.

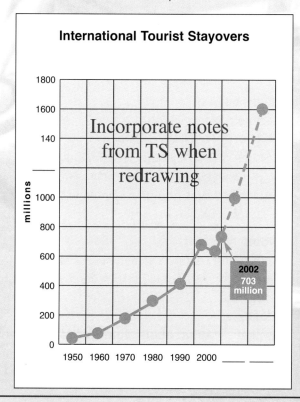

International Tourist Stayovers

Incorporate notes from TS when redrawing

2002
703 million

Skills Check

Understanding pros and cons

Lecturers often give you the **positive** and the **negative** sides of a theme. Sometimes they *tell* you that a point is positive or negative – e.g., 1 and 2 below.

Sometimes you have to *work out for yourself* if the point is ✓ or ✗. – e.g., 3.

Examples:

1 *Economists call this the Multiplier Effect, and it is the good side of tourism.* = ✓

2 *Of course, not all the extra spending benefits the local community.* = ✗

3 *Generally, jobs in tourism are unskilled and low-paid.* = ?

Organise your notes into two columns:

✓	✗
multiplier effect	not all $ → loc. comm.

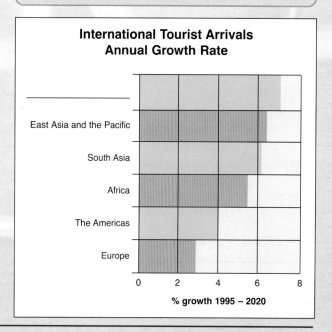

International Tourist Arrivals
Annual Growth Rate

% growth 1995 – 2020

Lesson 4: Applying new skills

A Match the adjective and noun to make a noun phrase from the lecture in Lessons 2 and 3. 🎧 Listen and check.

1 economic	community
2 internal	course
3 local	environment
4 tourist	government
5 different	impact
6 swimming	industry
7 golf	lifestyle
8 electricity	pool
9 national	supply
10 fragile	tourism

B In the lecture in Lessons 2 and 3, the lecturer asked the students to supply some information.
1 How did he ask? Complete the sentences and phrases in the speech bubbles.
2 What do you say if another student has given your answer?
3 Read the Skills Check. Check your ideas.

What do you _____?

Any other _____?

Anyone _____?

Come on, don't be _____.

C 🎧 Listen to each section from the second half of the lecture again.
1 Each time the lecturer asks you to contribute, think of something you could say. Make a note. Don't say anything until the teacher asks you.
2 Listen to other students' contributions. Make sure your contribution is still relevant.

D The lecturer ends by saying:

For all these reasons, tourism must be managed … and that's what you are here to learn about.

What do you think a course on Tourism Management should contain?

Skills Check

Contributing to discussions

Lecturers sometimes ask you to supply information or take part in a quick discussion.
You must listen carefully to the lecturer's question and to the contributions of other students.
Examples:
Lecturer: Which region is at the top of the growth graph? **What do you think?**
Student 1: Europe?
Lecturer: No, Europe's there already, isn't it? **Any other ideas?**
Student 2: Japan?
Lecturer: Japan's in East Asia and the Pacific. **Anyone else? Come on, don't be shy.**
Student 3: Is it the Middle East?
Lecturer: Absolutely.

Don't be frightened to contribute, but listen carefully to other contributions. Has someone already given your answer? If the lecturer chooses you in this case, explain the situation.
Example:
Lecturer: What is the financial value of this part of the leisure industry? What do you think?
Student 1: A billion dollars?
Lecturer: Anyone else?
Student 2: Ten billion dollars?
Lecturer: OK. Any other ideas? What about you? What do you think?
Student 3: **I was going to say** ten billion dollars.
Lecturer: OK.

Note:
Remember! Lecturers sometimes ask **rhetorical questions** (see Theme 5). They don't want you to contribute.
Example:
Lecturer: **What about domestic tourism?** This is where people visit tourist attractions in their own country.

In this theme you are going to listen to two lectures about food hygiene.

Lesson 1: Vocabulary

bacteria

Ⓐ 🔘 Listen to some words. Find and say a red word or phrase that is connected in some way to each word. Then explain the connection.

Example:

You hear *meat*. You say: '*Beef*, because *beef* is a kind of *meat*.' or
'*Protein*, because *beef* contains *protein*.'

Ⓑ Look at the quiz from a magazine. 🔘 Listen to two students doing the quiz.

Ⓒ Do the quiz in pairs. You might need some of the green words in your answers. (You will get the answers in the next lesson.)

SO *you think you know about ...*
Food hygiene

1. What makes food harmful?
2. How can you be sure that food is safe?
3. How do you know that food is unsafe?
4. What should you do if you are not sure about food?
5. How should you store fresh food?
6. How can you be sure that food is safe on a picnic?
7. What should you do before and after handling food?
8. What should you do with fruit and vegetables before eating them?
9. How should you defrost meat from a freezer?
10. What should you do after cooking soup in a microwave?

For answers, see page ...

beef *(n)*

carbohydrate *(n)*

dairy product *(n)*

date *(n)*

fish *(n)*

lamb *(n)*

mineral *(n)*

protein *(n)*

tomato/es *(n)*

vitamin *(n)*

bacterium/a *(n)*

defrost *(v)*

freezer *(n)*

handle *(v)*

harmful *(adj)*

microwave *(n)*

smell *(n)*

stir *(v)*

store *(v)*

throw away *(v)*

unsafe *(adj)*

use-by date *(n)*

Lesson 2: Listening review (1)

Ⓐ Look back at the quiz in Lesson 1. Think of an answer for each question.

Ⓑ In this course you have learnt to recognise signposts to help you organise your notes.
🔊 Listen to the introduction to the lecture. Complete the outline notes.

Ⓒ In this course you have learnt to make notes using abbreviations and symbols.
🔊 Listen to the first part of the lecture and make notes.

Ⓓ Decide if each of the statements below is true or false.
🔊 Listen again and check your answers.
1 You cannot see bacteria without a microscope.
2 All bacteria are harmful.
3 Some bacteria can kill you.
4 Four bacteria multiply to become six.
5 Bacteria die at less than 4°C.

> Food _____
> 1 Harmful food – three factors
>   1.1 bacteria
>   1.2 _____
>   1.3 _____
> 2 Looking after food
>   2.1 storing
>   2.2 _____
>   2.3 use-by date

Ⓔ In this course you have learnt to guess the spelling of proper nouns. You have also learnt to recognise digressions.
🔊 Listen to the second part of the lecture.
1 Make notes of the main points.
2 Guess the spelling of any proper nouns.
3 Do not make notes of the information in any digression.

Ⓕ In this course you have learnt to recognise rhetorical questions and to contribute to discussions during a lecture.
1 Complete the rhetorical questions (blue box) from the lecture so far.
2 How does the lecturer answer each question?
3 🔊 Listen to the third part of the lecture. Recognise rhetorical questions. Contribute to the discussion when the lecturer asks you to.

> When does food _____ harmful?
> How can you be _____ that food is safe?
> What is the correct _____ to handle food?

Ⓖ Do the quiz from Lesson 1 again. Use information from the lecture to answer the questions.

Lesson 3: Listening review (2)

A In this course you have learnt to recognise a lot of fixed phrases.

1 Complete each fixed phrase in the blue box with one word.

2 🔘 Listen and check your answers.

3 Choose five of the phrases. Think of a complete sentence with each phrase.

B In this course you have learnt to recognise signpost language.

1 🔘 Listen again to parts of the lecture in Lesson 2. Find a good way to continue in the yellow box.

2 🔘 Listen to the way each part continues and check your answers.

C In this course you have learnt to understand graphs in lectures. Study Figure 1, from a lecture.

1 What sentences do you expect to hear in the lecture?
Example: The figure for food poisoning cases in 1993 was just under 70,000.

2 Graphs do not tell you why things happened. Suggest possible reasons for the data in Figure 1.
Example: *Perhaps the number of cases rose in 1997 because there was a problem with meat or another food.*

Figure 1: Food poisoning cases in England and Wales

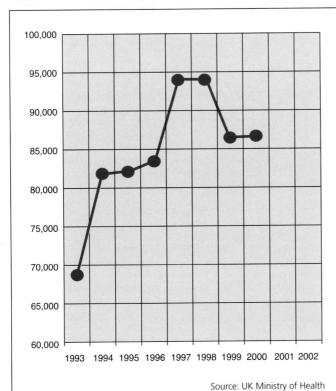

Source: UK Ministry of Health

- all over the _____
- cause and _____
- for thousands of _____
- getting back to the _____
- in other _____
- it all started _____
- it is fair to _____ that
- it is important to _____
- it is only _____ that
- let me say straight _____
- on the one _____
- so to sum _____
- the majority of _____
- the rest of her _____
- to put it another _____

- Firstly, there must be harmful bacteria or microorganisms in or on the food.
- handling it correctly.
- I went on a wadi trip and the host brought the food in shopping bags. Anyway, getting back to the point.
- if in doubt, throw it out!
- Most food that we buy in a shop is safe, but we must store it correctly and handle it correctly.
- Now let's consider handling food correctly.
- one bacterium becomes two, then four, then eight, and so on.
- the freezer is a wonderful invention that enables you to keep food like meat for several months without it going bad.
- the human body needs bacteria to work properly.
- we are going to look at some facts and figures on food poisoning.

Lesson 4: Listening review (3)

A What are the most common causes of accidental death? Number these causes in order.

_____ accidents with guns

_____ accidents with machinery

_____ drowning

_____ falls (from ladders, roofs, etc.)

_____ fires

_____ food poisoning

_____ getting something stuck in your throat

_____ mistakes by doctors / hospitals

_____ road accidents

_____ poisoning by gas

B You are going to hear another lecture about food hygiene.

🔊 Listen to the introduction to the lecture. Complete the graph with the missing information.

Figure 1: Most common causes of accidental death in the USA, 2002

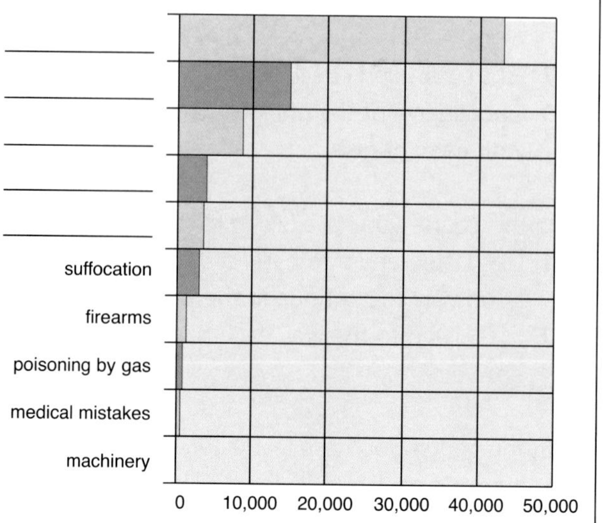

Source: Office of National Statistics

C In this course you have learnt to understand a speaker's argument.

1 Complete the introduction to this lecture with the phrases in the yellow box.

2 🔊 Listen again and check your answers.

| after all | it's true that | let me say straight away |
| OK, I hear you say | OK, they said | surely |

After the lecture, several students came up to me and asked how important this subject really was. _____, of course it was important to be careful with food, but you didn't have to go mad about it. _____, they didn't know anybody who had died from food poisoning. _____, you just got a stomachache and that was that? Well, I'm pleased that your experience of food poisoning has not been too bad, but _____ that food poisoning *is* a very serious danger, especially in a hot country, and you must constantly guard against it. _____, food poisoning is dangerous, but it isn't very common. _____ it isn't the *most* common cause of accidental death. In most countries, that is road accidents.

D In this course you have learnt to predict what a speaker is going to say.

🔊 Listen to the final part of the lecture. When the lecturer stops, predict the next word. Then listen and check your ideas.

E What is the lecturer's Food Code?

1 Make some notes.

2 Explain how to do each point and the reasons behind it.

THEME 1
Education, How Do We Learn?

forget *(v)*

memorable *(adj)*

memory *(n)*

remember *(v)*

behave *(v)*

behaviour *(n)*

experience *(n)*

learning *(n)*

observation *(n)*

observe *(v)*

theory/ies *(n)*

THEME 2
Daily Life, Growing Up

accept *(v)*

attitude *(n)*

behaviour *(n)*

colleague *(n)*

criticise *(v)*

neighbourhood *(n)*

occasion *(n)*

optimistic *(adj)*

trust *(v)*

adolescence *(n)*

adolescent *(n)*

adulthood *(n)*

baby *(n)*

conflict *(n)*

develop *(v)*

grow up *(v)*

identity *(n)*

infancy *(n)*

infant *(n)*

middle-aged *(adj)*

THEME 3
Work and Business, Why Do People Work Hard?

balance *(v)*

current *(adj)*

equal *(v)*

equation *(n)*

increase *(v)*

previous *(adj)*

side *(n)*

employee *(n)*

industrial *(adj)*

need *(n)*

produce *(v)*

production *(n)*

rest break *(n)*

team *(n)*

working hours *(n)*

THEME 4
Science and Nature, Tornadoes and Hurricanes

around / about (= approx) *(prep)*

desert *(n)*

expand *(n)*

occupy *(v)*

plant *(n)*

surface *(n)*

the Earth *(n)*

duration *(n)*

formation *(n)*

lightning *(n)*

occur *(v)*

origin *(n)*

reach (= max. amount) *(v)*

sandstorm *(n)*

speed *(n)*

thunder *(n)*

timing *(n)*

THEME 5 The Physical World, Natural Disasters	**THEME 6** Culture and Civilization, What Is Society?	**THEME 7** They Made Our World, The Greatest Advance in History	**THEME 8** Art and Literature, Gulliver and Robinson Crusoe
agriculture *(n)*	birth *(n)*	build *(v)*	begin *(v)*
climate *(n)*	customs *(n)*		belong *(v)*
difference *(n)*		device *(n)*	buy *(v)*
different *(adj)*	get married *(v)*		disappear *(v)*
industry *(n)*	marriage *(n)*	idea *(n)*	explore *(v)*
population *(n)*	marry *(v)*		hear *(v)*
similarities *(n)*		inventor *(n)*	land *(v)*
temperature *(n)*	wedding *(n)*		let *(v)*
the economy *(n)*	achieve *(v)*	replace *(v)*	light *(v)*
the same *(adj)*	achievement *(n)*		need *(v)*
trading partner *(n)*	advance *(n)*	technology *(n)*	search *(v)*
damage *(n and v)*	culture *(n)*	antibiotics *(n)*	see *(v)*
death *(n)*		engine *(n)*	sell *(v)*
erupt *(v)*	individual *(n)*		spend *(v)*
fire *(n)*	relationship *(n)*	preservation *(n)*	think *(v)*
natural disaster *(n)*	social *(adj)*		trick *(v)*
rock *(n)*	society *(n)*	printing *(n)*	adventure *(n)*
shake *(v)*	sociology *(n)*	wheel *(n)*	allegory *(n)*
tidal wave *(n)*			author *(n)*
			base (on) *(v)*
			criticism *(n)*
			critic *(n)*
			hero *(n)*
			popular *(adj)*
			represent *(v)*
			version *(n)*

THEME 9
Sports and Leisure, $5,000,000,000,000 p.a.

athlete (n)

compete (v)

event (n)

fit (adj)

physical fitness (n)

practice (n)

practise (v)

race (n)

sportsman (n)

sportswoman (n)

throw (v)

train (v)

abroad (adj)

growth (n)

impact (n)

international (adj)

lifestyle (n)

negative (adj)

positive (adj)

pros and cons (n)

sightseeing (n)

tourism (n)

tourist (n)

THEME 10
Nutrition and Health, Food – The New Poison?

beef (n)

carbohydrate (n)

dairy product (n)

date (n)

fish (n)

lamb (n)

mineral (n)

protein (n)

tomato/es (n)

vitamin (n)

bacterium/a (n)

defrost (v)

freezer (n)

handle (v)

harmful (adj)

microwave (n)

smell (n)

stir (v)

store (v)

throw away (v)

unsafe (adj)

use-by date (n)

---

abroad (adj)

accept (v)

achieve (v)

achievement (n)

adolescence (n)

adolescent (n)

adulthood (n)

advance (n)

adventure (n)

agriculture (n)

allegory (n)

antibiotics (n)

around / about (= approx) (prep)

athlete (n)

attitude (n)

author (n)

baby (n)

bacterium/a (n)

balance (v)

base (on) (v)

beef (n)

begin (v)

behave (v)

behaviour (n)

belong (v)

birth (n)

build (v)

buy (v)

carbohydrate (n)

climate (n)

colleague (n)

compete (v)

conflict (n)

critic (n)

criticise (v)

criticism (n)

culture (n)

current (adj)

customs (n)

dairy product (n)

damage (n and v)

date (n)

death (n)

defrost (v)

desert (n)

---

develop (v)

device (n)

difference (n)

different (adj)

disappear (v)

duration (n)

employee (n)

engine (n)

equal (v)

equation (n)

erupt (v)

event (n)

expand (n)

experience (n)

explore (v)

fire (n)

fish (n)

fit (adj)

forget (v)

formation (n)

freezer (n)

get married (v)

grow up (v)

growth (n)

handle (v)

harmful (adj)

hear (v)

hero (n)

idea (n)

identity (n)

impact (n)

increase (v)

individual (n)

industrial (adj)

industry (n)

infancy (n)

infant (n)

international (adj)

inventor (n)

lamb (n)

land (v)

learning (n)

let (v)

lifestyle (n)

light (v)

lightning (n)

marriage (n)
marry (v)
memorable (adj)
memory (n)
microwave (n)
middle-aged (adj)
mineral (n)
natural disaster (n)
need (n)
need (v)
negative (adj)
neighbourhood (n)
observation (n)
observe (v)
occasion (n)
occupy (v)
occur (v)
optimistic (adj)
origin (n)
physical fitness (n)
plant (n)
popular (adj)
population (n)
positive (adj)
practice (n)
practise (v)
preservation (n)
previous (adj)
printing (n)
produce (v)
production (n)
pros and cons (n)
protein (n)
race (n)
reach (= max. amount) (v)
relationship (n)
remember (v)
replace (v)
represent (v)
rest break (n)
rock (n)
sandstorm (n)
search (v)
see (v)

sell (v)
shake (v)
side (n)
sightseeing (n)
similarities (n)
smell (n)
social (adj)
society (n)
sociology (n)
speed (n)
spend (v)
sportsman (n)
sportswoman (n)
stir (v)
store (v)
surface (n)
team (n)
technology (n)
temperature (n)
the Earth (n)
the economy (n)
the same (n)
theory/ies (n)
think (v)
throw (v)
throw away (v)
thunder (n)
tidal wave (n)
timing (n)
tomato/es (n)
tourism (n)
tourist (n)
trading partner (n)
train (v)
trick (v)
trust (v)
unsafe (adj)
use-by date (n)
version (n)
vitamin (n)
wedding (n)
wheel (n)
working hours (n)

Tapescript

Presenter:	Skills in English Listening: Level 3 Theme 1: Education, How Do We Learn? Lesson 1: Vocabulary **B Listen to a short text with the green words. Then complete the text with one of the words in each space.**
Voice:	What is learning? Scientists define learning as a change of behaviour. But how do we learn? Nobody knows for sure, but there are many theories from psychologists and philosophers. Some say, 'People learn from experience. For example, a baby cries and his mother gives him food. He learns that certain behaviour is useful.' Other people think that we learn by observation. They say, 'We look around at the world. We observe other people. We see how they behave. We copy them.'
Presenter:	**D 2 Listen and number the words you hear.**
Voice:	observe experience behave behaviour learning theory observation
Presenter:	**Lesson 2: Listening** **B 2 Listen to the introduction. Complete the outline.**
Female lecturer:	How do we learn? This seems like a simple question, but there is no simple answer. In the next two lectures, we are going to look at theories of learning. This week I'm going to talk about theories from the distant past. Firstly, theories from Ancient Greece. Next, theories from Islamic scholars. Finally, a very famous theory from Russia. Next week, I'm going to describe the work of two Americans, Skinner and Watson, in the 20th century.
Presenter:	**C Listen to the first part of the lecture.**
Female lecturer:	So, first, to Ancient Greece. The Greek philosopher Plato – that's P-L-A-T-O – lived from 427 BCE to about 347 BCE. He believed that learning was just memory. We have an experience. Maybe it's good. Maybe it's bad. Maybe we remember. Maybe we forget. If we remember later, that's learning by experience. For example, a child touches a fire and burns himself. He remembers next time and doesn't touch the fire.
Presenter:	**D Listen to the rest of the lecture. Complete Table 1.**
Female lecturer:	Plato's student, Aristotle, lived from 384 BCE to 322 BCE. Aristotle is spelt A-R-I-S-T-O-T-L-E. He believed, like Plato, that we learn by doing things. But he went further. He believed that people learn when they see the cause of things, when they understand why something happens. For example, a child touches a fire and burns himself. Later he touches a match and burns himself. He sees a pattern: hot things burn you. After the child sees the pattern, he does not touch any hot things, including irons and boiling

water – things that haven't burnt him in the past. Next, the Islamic scholars. A lot of Greek learning was lost to the Western World in the 5th century AD. But Islamic philosophers and scientists translated the works of Plato and Aristotle. Scholars like Al Farabi in the 9th century AD, Ibn Sina in the 10th century and Ibn Rushd in the 12th century carried forward Aristotle's ideas. They also added theories of their own. A common theme in Islamic science is that learning comes from studying nature. Nowadays, we call this 'learning by observation'. The child observes another child touching a fire. He sees that the other child is burnt. He does not touch the fire himself. Finally, to Russia and a very important theory. In the 19th century, a Russian psychologist called Ivan Pavlov – that's P-A-V-L-O-V – started to study dogs. He was not interested in learning. He wanted to know why a dog's mouth produced saliva when it got its food. Saliva is necessary for the correct digestion of the food. But how did the dogs know to produce the saliva at the right time? First, Pavlov thought it was the smell of the food. But the dogs produced saliva when they saw the person who brought the food, even if the person had no food at the time. Pavlov decided to do an experiment. He gave a dog some meat powder every few minutes. Every time the dog licked the powder, Pavlov rang a bell. After a short time, the dog salivated when it heard the bell, without getting the food. He reversed the experiment. He rang a bell but didn't give the dog any food. After a short time, the dog stopped salivating when it heard the bell.

What is the connection between Pavlov's dogs and human learning? Pavlov's experiment led to a new theory about how we learn. Scientists said that events in our environment can change the way we behave. In other words, we learn to behave in a particular way because of the way people and things behave around us. Pavlov called this process 'conditioning'. Pavlov's theory says a child can become frightened of something without having direct experience and without observing someone else having the experience. So, for example, if a mother sees her child is going to touch a fire, she shouts 'No!' She frightens the child. The child connects the fear and the fire, even though he did not get burnt himself or see anyone else getting burnt.

Presenter: **Lesson 3: Checking skills**
C 3 Listen and check your ideas.

Female lecturer: Plato's student, Aristotle, lived from 384 BCE to 322 BCE. Aristotle is spelt A-R-I-S-T-O-T-L-E. He believed, like Plato, that we learn by doing things. But he went further. He believed that people learn when they see the cause of things, when they understand why something happens. For example, a child touches a fire and burns himself. Later he touches a match and burns himself. He sees a pattern: hot things burn you. After the child sees the pattern, he does not touch any hot things, including irons and boiling water – things that haven't burnt him in the past.

Presenter: **D 2 Listen and check.**
Female lecturer: He gave a dog some meat powder every few minutes. Every time the dog licked the powder, Pavlov rang a bell. After a short time, the dog salivated when it heard the bell, without getting the food. He reversed the experiment. He rang a bell but didn't give the dog any food. After a short time, the dog stopped salivating when it heard the bell.

Presenter: **E 2 Listen and check.**
Female lecturer: What is the connection between Pavlov's dogs and human learning? Pavlov's experiment led to a new theory about how we learn. Scientists said that events in our environment can change the way we behave. Pavlov called this process 'conditioning'. Pavlov's theory says a child can become frightened of something without having direct experience and without observing someone else having the experience.

Presenter: **Lesson 4: Applying skills**
B 2 Listen to the introduction. Make outline notes for the lecture.
Female lecturer: This is the second of two lectures on the topic: How do we learn? Last week, we talked about a number of theories through history. Firstly, we heard about the theories of Plato and Aristotle in Ancient Greece. Then we learnt about the theories of the Islamic scholars Al-Farabi, Ibn Sina and Ibn Rushd in the Arab World. Finally, I talked about the psychologist, Pavlov, and his famous experiment in 19th-century Russia. We learnt that philosophers believe we learn by remembering, or by understanding why, or by observing or through conditioning.

This week, we are going to look at some theories from the 20th century. Firstly, I am going to talk about the theory of an American called Watson. Then, I will describe the theory of another American called Skinner. His ideas had a big effect on the way people started to teach foreign languages.

Presenter: **C Listen to the first part of the lecture. What is the main point of this part?**
Female lecturer: John Watson accepted the ideas of Pavlov. He believed that you could extend them to human beings. He believed that experiences in people's lives changed their behaviour. He said this was much more important than any natural behaviour that people inherited from their parents.

Watson conducted a famous experiment in 1919 and 1920. He used a baby called Albert in his experiment. He gave baby Albert a white rat. Albert tried to touch the rat. Watson made a loud noise just behind the baby's ear. Albert started to cry. Every time he tried to touch the rat, Watson made a loud noise and frightened the baby. Every time, the baby started to cry. Soon, Albert cried when the rat appeared. In fact, he cried when he saw anything that looked like a rat – a furry toy or a fur coat. Watson's experiment proved that conditioning worked in people as well as animals.

Presenter: **D Listen to the second part of the lecture. Connect the pictures and explain the main ideas in this part.**
Female lecturer: Watson's work was important. However, the work of another American, B.F. Skinner, was much more important in the history of education. Skinner worked in a laboratory in the 1940s. He also knew about the work of Pavlov. Pavlov showed that a new stimulus, like a bell ringing, can make an animal produce *existing* behaviour, like salivating for food. Skinner thought, 'Can I teach animals to learn *new* behaviour through conditioning?'

First, he did experiments with rats. He taught rats to

get through very complicated mazes to find food. They had to push buttons and move levers to open doors. At the end of the maze, they found food. Then Skinner did something amazing. He taught pigeons to play table tennis. How did he do this? He watched the pigeons very closely. Every time they did something like push a table tennis ball with their beaks, he gave them some food. Finally, he conditioned the pigeons to play table tennis to get food.

Presenter: E **Listen to the third part of the lecture. Number these events in order.**

Female lecturer: Skinner worked with animals, not people, but he believed that his results could apply to people as well. In particular, he said that conditioning pigeons to play table tennis was like conditioning children to speak their own language. For example, a baby makes a sound when his mother comes in the room. The mother thinks the sound is like the word 'Mummy'. She repeats it. This happens hundreds of times. Finally, the child says 'Mummy' when his mother comes into the room.

Presenter: Theme 2: Daily Life, Growing Up
Lesson 1: Vocabulary
B **Listen to a short text with the green words. Then complete the text with one of the words in each space. Make any necessary changes.**

Voice: Do you sometimes ask yourself: 'Who am I?' If you do, you are normal. Indeed, psychologists say that we ask ourselves this question throughout our lives. The meaning of the question changes as we grow up. Babies ask, 'Who am I? Is this hand part of me, or part of you?' Infants ask, 'Who am I? My parents choose my clothes, my food, my school, my bedtime.' Adolescents ask, 'Who am I? A nice person or a nasty one?' Middle-aged adults ask, 'Who am I? What have I done with my life?'
We ask the question because, according to Erik Erikson (see Lesson 4), at every age there is an identity crisis – a conflict or battle between who we are and who we would like to be. At every age we find different answers, because, according to Piaget (see Lesson 2), our brains develop in a predictable way through infancy and adolescence to adulthood.

Presenter: C 2 **Listen and check your ideas.**
Voice: 1 birth
2 infancy
3 childhood
4 adolescence
5 adulthood
6 middle age
7 death

Presenter: Lesson 2: Listening
B **Listen to the introduction. Make a set of outline notes for this week's lecture.**

Male lecturer: In these two lectures, we are going to look at two theories of child development. Firstly, this week, I'm going to look at Jean Piaget. That's ET at the end because he was a French speaker. Next week, I'll talk about the life and work of Erik Erikson.
OK, so this week, I'm going to talk about Piaget's life and how he developed his ideas. Then I'm going to explain to you Piaget's four stages of child development.

Presenter: D 1 **Listen to the first part of the lecture.**
Male : lecturer

Jean Piaget was born in Switzerland on August 9, 1896. When he was 11 years old, he wrote a scientific essay about a small bird. This was the start of a long career of research and writing that included more than 60 books and hundreds of articles.
After birds, he became interested in shellfish. He published many articles on the subject while he was still at school.
After he left school, he studied natural sciences at the University of Neuchâtel – that's N-E-U-C-H-A-T-E-L. He got his PhD and then left Switzerland to work in a school in France. This was the beginning of his work with children, which continued for the rest of his life. He developed a test for intelligence in five- to eight-year olds, and he became interested in the way that brains develop, or what he called 'the biological explanation of knowledge'. He discovered that children at a certain age could solve problems that children at an earlier age could never solve. He decided to find out more.
In 1921, he returned to Switzerland to become director of studies at an institute in Geneva. He got married two years later, and the couple had three children. This was important in his professional as well as his social life. He studied the development of the three children closely, from infancy to adulthood. During the next 40 years, he held a succession of important posts in universities and research institutes. He died in Geneva on September 16, 1980.

Presenter: D 3 **Listen again. Put the notes on Piaget's life, work and ideas together.**
[REPEAT OF LESSON 2 EXERCISE D1]

Presenter: E **Listen to the second part of the lecture.**
Male lecturer:

For the whole of his adult life, Piaget kept asking the same question: 'How does knowledge grow?' He had the idea, which was unusual at the time, of actually talking to children and finding out their ideas. For example, there is one story about a conversation with a five-year-old girl. He asked her: 'What makes the wind?'
The child replied: 'The trees.'
'How do you know?'
'I saw them waving their arms.'
'How does that make the wind?'
'Like this. Only they are bigger. And there are lots of trees.'
'What makes the wind on the ocean?'
'It blows there from the land. No. It's the waves ...'
Piaget said, 'Children only really understand things that they invent themselves. If we try to teach them something too quickly, we stop them reinventing it themselves.'
In another experiment, Piaget told lots of children the same story. He said, 'Imagine that one boy is washing up after dinner and he breaks two cups. Imagine that another boy asks his mother, 'Can I have some chocolate?' and the mother says, 'No'. Then this boy tries to get the chocolate and he breaks a cup. Which child is naughtier?' Young children always answered, 'The first child, because he broke two cups. The other child only broke one cup.' Older children said, 'The second child, because he was doing something naughty when he broke the cup. The first child was trying to be helpful.' This shows that ideas of right and wrong change as children grow up.
Piaget decided, after many years, that knowledge

grows in a predictable way, from simple ideas to more complex ones. He concluded that the brain of an infant is different from the brain of a child, and different from the brain of an adolescent or an adult. Piaget's work has influenced people all over the world in many fields, including psychology, sociology and education. His theories of child development are still the basis of most thinking in this area.

So what did Piaget actually discover? He found that there are four major stages of development, although each of these stages has many subdivisions.

Presenter: **F 2 Listen to the third part of the lecture and check your ideas.**

Male lecturer: The first stage lasts from birth up to about 18 months or two years. He called this stage the sensorimotor stage, that's S-E-N-S-O-R-I-M-O-T-O-R. Babies do not know how things will react, and so they are always experimenting – shaking things, putting things in their mouths, throwing. They are learning by experience. We sometimes call this kind of learning trial and error.

The second stage lasts from 18 to 24 months to 7 years. Piaget called this stage pre-operational. Pre means before, so this is before operational thought. In this stage, children learn to speak. They can pretend and they can understand past and future. However, they cannot understand cause-and-effect. In other words, they cannot understand 'if I do this, this will happen'.

The third stage is from 7 to 12 years. Piaget called this the stage of concrete operational thought. Concrete, spelt C-O-N-C-R-E-T-E, in this case, means real, not abstract. At this stage, children can understand that real things stay the same, even if you move them around. For example, a litre of water is a litre of water in a small bottle or a big bottle.

The final stage of child development happens after about 12 years old. Piaget called this the stage of formal operational thought. Formal in this case means not real, but abstract. At this stage, children can understand algebra – for example, a + b = c, and they can understand hypotheses and abstract ideas like fairness and justice.

So, to sum up, Piaget believed that all children go through these four stages more or less at the same age. Although some people today criticise his ideas, he is still widely regarded as the greatest developmental psychologist of the 20th century. Einstein called his discovery of developmental stages 'so simple that only a genius could have thought of it.' OK. Next week, Erik Erikson and some more ideas on child development.

Presenter: **G Listen to the third part again. Complete the table.**
[REPEAT OF LESSON 2 EXERCISE F2]

Presenter: **Lesson 3: Learning new skills**
B 3 Listen and check your ideas.

Voice: a cause and effect
b in other words
c learning by experience
d life and work
e more or less
f past and future
g professional and social
h right and wrong
i so to sum up

j trial and error
k all over the world
l the rest of his life

Presenter: **Lesson 4: Applying new skills**
A 2 Listen and check your ideas.

Voice: a career
b research
c explanation
d knowledge
e infancy
f adulthood
g professional
h social
i experience
j effect
k algebra
l react
m error
n trial
o theory

Presenter: **B You are going to hear the second lecture about child development. Listen to the introduction. Make a set of outline notes.**

Male lecturer: Last week, we talked about the work of Jean Piaget on child development. This week, we are going to look at the life and work of another famous person in this field, Erik Erikson – that's E-R-I-K E-R-I-K-S-O-N. First I'm going to tell you a little about his life, because it is possible that his life influenced his work. Then I'm going to describe his theories of child development.

Presenter: **C Listen to the first part of the lecture.**

Male lecturer: Erikson was born in Germany on June 15th, 1902. There is no record of the name of his real father. In 1905, when Erik was three, his mother married Erik's doctor, Theodor Homberger – that's H-O-M-B-E-R-G-E-R. So he grew up as Erik Homberger.

Erikson left school in about 1920. He became an artist and then a teacher. Then he studied child psychology in Austria. During this time he got married. He and his wife emigrated to the United States in 1933. He taught at Yale and Harvard, on the East Coast. In 1939, he moved to California, on the West Coast, to teach at the university at Berkeley. He began to study groups of Native American children. He studied the way they developed the values of their parents.

Also in 1939, Erik Homberger became an American citizen and changed his family name to Erikson. There is an interesting story about this. Erik never knew his real father, but at some point he became aware that his real name was not Homberger. His mother refused to give him any information about his real father. For some reason, Erikson started to believe that he was the son of a royal prince from Denmark. Is that why he gave himself a Danish family name? And did this confusion about his own identity lead to Erik's interest in identity in children?

Erikson moved back to the East Coast of the United States in 1950 and continued working and teaching there until he retired in 1970. He died on May 12th, 1994.

Presenter: **D Listen to the second part of the lecture.**

Male lecturer: Erikson published his first book in 1950. It was called *Childhood and Society*. The book is still widely read in the field of psychoanalysis. In this book, Erikson developed his theory of the identity crisis. This is the idea that a child must find its own identity as it moves through various stages of development. It is clear that Erikson did not find his full identity. Even the simplest personal questions seemed to cause a problem for him. There are many stories about this. For example, if someone asked Erikson 'How are you?' he often turned to his wife and said, 'Well, Joan. How are we?' But perhaps the most surprising story is about Erikson and food. If someone gave Erikson some food that he wasn't expecting, he sometimes turned to his wife and asked, 'Do I want this, Joan?'

Presenter: **E Listen to the third part of the lecture. Complete the table of Erikson's stages of development.**

Male lecturer:
What about his work and ideas? Erikson identified eight stages of development, through childhood and adult life. We are only going to look at the first five stages, because these lectures are about child development, not adult development. At each stage, Erikson said that there is a conflict, a battle, a war, with a good result and a bad result.

The first stage lasts for the first one or two years of life. It is the stage of trust versus mistrust. An infant learns to trust his or her parents and adults in general – or learns that adults are not to be trusted. Trust versus mistrust.

The second stage is from about two years to about four years. It is the stage of self-confidence versus shame. A young child learns to be confident in his ability to do things by himself – or he learns to be ashamed of his failure to do things. Unfortunately for parents, the confident child is also developing willpower, and often refuses to obey. This is difficult for the parents but is part of the child's social development. So the second stage is self-confidence versus shame.

The third stage is from about four to entry into school at five or six. It is the stage of initiative versus guilt. Perhaps those words are new to you. Initiative is spelt I-N-I-T-I-A-T-I-V-E, and it means doing something yourself, without being told to do it. Guilt – G-U-I-L-T – means feeling bad about something you have done wrong. At this stage, the child learns to take initiative, to cooperate with other children, to lead and to follow. The child also learns to imagine and to pretend. This is the wonderful period of make-believe. So, initiative is the good result. Or the child feels guilty and refuses to take part in games, does not play with other children and does not develop play skills or imagination. So this stage is initiative versus guilt.

The fourth stage occurs during the early years of schooling. It is the stage of structured play versus inferiority. Structured play means playing team games with other children. Inferiority – I-N-F-E-R-I-O-R-I-T-Y – means feeling that you are not as good as other children. The child learns to play structured games that involve teamwork. The child also learns self-discipline and manages his or her own homework. A child who has come through stages 1, 2 and 3 successfully will have little difficulty with this stage – he will trust adults and work with initiative. However, the child who has had problems at earlier stages will fail at this stage, too. He will mistrust adults and not take charge of his own life. He will feel shame, guilt and inferiority.

The fifth stage is the stage of adolescence, from 13 or 14 to about 20. It is the stage of identity – of knowing who you are – versus diffusion – that's D-I-F-F-U-S-I-O-N – as Erikson calls it – not knowing who you are. The successful adolescent learns self-confidence rather than self-consciousness, which means being embarrassed about the way you look, the way you speak, the way you dress, etc. Erikson believed that there are three more stages that occur in adulthood. As we are talking about child development, I am not going to discuss those here. Erikson's theory is that a child needs to learn to socialise – to become part of the society he or she lives in. The job of a parent and a teacher is to help the child to move from being helpless and centred on him or herself, to being a part of society, but also to be an independent thinker.

Presenter: **F These statements are true or probably true. Listen to the lecture again and find evidence.**
[REPEAT OF LESSON 4 EXERCISES B, C, D AND E]

Presenter: **Theme 3: Work and Business, Why Do People Work Hard?**
Lesson 1: Vocabulary
A 3 Listen and check your answers.

Voice:
We often use equations in business. For example, the price of something in a shop usually equals the cost to make it plus some profit for the company. We can write this as an equation: cost + profit = price. Both sides of an equation must be the same. In other words, they must balance. So if the cost is $20 and the profit is $2, the price must be $22. What happens if the cost increases? We can use our equation to make sure the profit stays the same. If the previous cost was $20 and the current cost is $22, then the new price must be $24.

Presenter: **B 3 Listen and check your answers.**
Voice:
Equation 1: salary per hour x working hours per week = total salary per week
Example: $10 x 48 hours = $480

Equation 2: working hours per day - rest breaks = total working hours per day
Example: 8 hours - 1.5 hours = 6.5 hours

Equation 3: managers + workers = employees
Example: 5 managers + 100 workers = 105 employees

Presenter: **C 2 Listen to each sentence. What form of the word do you hear? What does the word mean in this situation?**
Voice:
a This is Mr Jones. He is the production manager.
b Good morning, Mr. Jones. What do you actually produce here?
c This is the industrial part of the city. All the factories are here.
d The workers have started to work as a team. They are producing a lot more now.
e We all have a number of needs. We need food and drink and love, for example.

Presenter: **D 2 Listen and check your ideas.**
Voice:
balance
current
equal
equation

increase
previous
employee
industrial
produce
production
working

Presenter: **Lesson 2: Listening**
C Listen to the introduction.

Female lecturer: This week and next week, I am going to talk about ideas in the field of Industrial Psychology. We know what psychology means – it is the study of how the brain works, of how people think. So what is Industrial Psychology? It is the study of the way people think about work and the effects of working conditions on productivity. Productivity is the amount of work that a person does in one time period, say one day. So for example, if one worker makes five items in one day and another worker makes six items, the second worker has a higher productivity than the first worker.

This week, I'm going to talk about the experiment that started Industrial Psychology and the conclusions that the researcher, Elton Mayo, reached about the results. Next week, I'm going to describe the theories of two writers in this field, Maslow and Herzberg.

Presenter: **D 2 Listen to the first part of the lecture. Follow the suggestions in the Skills Check Reminder.**

Female lecturer: It all started with a series of experiments at a factory in Chicago in the USA. The factory was called the Hawthorne Works. The experiments were carried out by Elton Mayo. He was an Australian, born on the 26th December, 1880. He moved to the UK in 1901, and then, in 1923, he went to the USA to teach at the University of Pennsylvania. Later, he became a professor at Harvard Business School. He became interested in the effect of working conditions on productivity. He decided to conduct some experiments. There was nothing very original about the experiments themselves but the results form the basis of Industrial Psychology to this day. Between 1924 and 1927, Mayo conducted experiments at the Hawthorne Works. He wondered if the level of light in the factory affected the productivity of the workers. He experimented with the lighting levels for three years, but he found no change in productivity.

Mayo then decided to look at the effect of tiredness on productivity. He wondered if productivity increased if you gave workers regular rest breaks or if you reduced the length of the working day. I don't know if you have ever been into a factory. I remember once I had to visit a factory. It was incredibly noisy and, of course, noise all day makes you tired. So it was a reasonable assumption that factory workers would be tired.

So, anyway, getting back to the point … between 1927 and 1932, Mayo conducted another experiment with a group of six girls in the Hawthorne Works. During those five years, Mayo and his researchers observed the girls at work and made changes to their rest breaks and their working hours. After each change, a researcher talked to the girls about the changes and listened to any complaints they had.

Presenter: **E Listen to the second part of the lecture, which gives details of the experiment.**

Female lecturer: Before the experiment started, the girls worked a 48 hour week. They had no rest periods during the day. They did not have a specific target for productivity, but on average, each girl produced 2,400 items a week.

Mayo introduced five-minute rest breaks, one in the morning and one in the afternoon. Productivity went up.

Mayo lengthened the rest breaks to ten minutes each. Productivity went up sharply.

Mayo introduced another four rest breaks, but the girls complained that their work rhythm was broken, and productivity went down slightly. These extra rest breaks were removed and productivity went up again. The girls were allowed to leave at 4.30 p.m. instead of 5.00 p.m. Productivity went up.

Then they were allowed to leave at 4.00 p.m. They were now working one hour a day less in total, but productivity did not go down.

Mayo concluded that tiredness did have an effect on productivity. He believed, at this point, that a shorter working day and regular rest breaks were the key to increasing productivity.

Presenter: **F Listen to the third part. Each time the lecturer stops, answer her question.**

Female lecturer: Before he closed the experiment, however, he decided to do one final thing. It is the thing that any good researcher would do in the circumstances. What did he decide to do? [PAUSE] He took all the changes away, but continued to observe the girls and talk to them. The girls went back to the same conditions as before the experiment started – a 48-hour week, no rest breaks. What happened? [PAUSE] Productivity went up again. In fact, at this point, the girls reached an all-time record of over 3,000 items per week. How can the results be explained? [PAUSE]

Presenter: **G Listen to the fourth part. What is the Hawthorne effect?**

Female lecturer: Mayo concluded that this is what happened: during the experiments, the six girls became a team. They realised that the management was interested in their work and listened to their complaints. They also realised that the amount of work they did – their productivity – was noticed. Mayo decided that productivity is affected by the amount that a worker is involved in the production process. Before the experiment started, nobody talked to the girls about their work. They felt they were just part of the factory machine. They did not feel valued. They did their work, but they did not do anything extra. When Mayo's researchers started to talk to them about their work, they felt that someone was noticing them as people. They felt valued. They did their work better because now they were putting extra effort into it. This discovery – that workers need to feel valued as people – is so important in the field of Industrial Psychology that it has a name, taken from the factory. When workers increase productivity because managers value their work, it is called the Hawthorne Effect. One other point came out of the experiment. Mayo noticed that, although all the girls were making the same item, they each had their own particular way of doing it. To put it another way, they each had a personal way to make a boring job a little bit more interesting. Mayo realised that people need to organise their own work in a way that will be interesting to them. There's a funny story about this. A man was visiting a factory where they make jam tarts. You know, they are little pieces of pastry with some jam on them. And he spoke to one of the girls who was operating a machine. He said, 'What do you do?' And she said, 'I push this button and the strawberry jam comes out of here.' And he said, 'But doesn't that get boring?' And she said, 'No. When I get bored, I push that button instead and make some tarts with *raspberry* jam.'

Mayo wrote about the results of the Hawthorne experiments in a book published in 1933. It was called *The Human Problems of an Industrial Civilization*. He went on to write two other books, in 1939 and 1947. He died on 1st September, 1949. So we have heard about Elton Mayo and the Hawthorne Effect, the discovery that really started the idea of Industrial Psychology – or the way that people think about work.

Next week, I'm going to talk about two people and their theories about Industrial Psychology.

Presenter: **Lesson 3: Learning new skills**
A 2 Listen and check your ideas.
Voice: it all started with
to this day
in fact
in the circumstances
in other words
getting back to the point
on average
in total
at work
for example
to put it another way

Presenter: **D 5 Listen to this part of the lecture again.**
Female lecturer: Mayo then decided to look at the effect of tiredness on productivity. He wondered if productivity increased if you gave workers regular rest breaks or if you reduced the length of the working day. I don't know if you have ever been into a factory. I remember once I had to visit a factory. It was incredibly noisy and, of course, noise all day makes you tired. So it was a reasonable assumption that factory workers would be tired.
So, anyway, getting back to the point …

Presenter: **Lesson 4: Applying new skills**
B Listen to the introduction.
Female lecturer: Last week, I talked about the start of Industrial Psychology, which is the study of how people think about work. I described the experiments of Elton Mayo at the Hawthorne Works, and the Hawthorne Effect, which says that people work better when they feel valued.
This week, two more writers in the field of Industrial Psychology. But before that, I'm going to mention the thing they have in common: motivation. In the end, Industrial Psychology is all about motivation at work. What motivates people to work hard – or not to work hard?
OK, so first, motivation. What is it? One definition is: *a way of satisfying needs through action and behaviour*. In other words, we need something, like money or food, and we try to get it. We are motivated by our needs. Researchers have discovered that different things motivate different people. Some

people are motivated by very strange things. I remember once I met a boy who collected train numbers. Yes, that's right. The numbers of trains. Trains all look the same in Britain, but each one has an identification number. This boy travelled to railway stations and stood for hours writing down the train numbers in a notebook. If I said to most boys, 'Go and write down train numbers,' they would be very bored. But this boy was motivated to do it for fun. Sorry. Where was I? Oh yes. Motivation. Different things motivate different people, so managers must understand the theories of motivation to get the best out of their employees.

Presenter: **D Listen to the first part of the lecture. Make notes on the life of Maslow.**
Female lecturer: Right. So, let's look at some of the theories. Firstly, we have Abraham Maslow, spelt M-A-S-L-O-W. Maslow was born on April 1, 1908, in New York. He was one of seven children born to uneducated Russian parents. His mother and father pushed him very hard to succeed. He went to university in New York for some time and studied law. While he was still a student, he got married and moved to Wisconsin to continue his studies at the university there. He switched from law to psychology and got his BA in 1930, his MA in 1931 and his PhD three years later. He went back to New York to work as a teacher at a college. He wrote several books, including *Motivation and Personality* in 1943. In this book, he described his most famous theory – the hierarchy of needs. Maslow retired to California in his early 60s, and died there on June 8th, 1970.

Presenter: **F Listen to the second part of the lecture. Check your answers to Exercise E.**
Female lecturer: As I just said, Maslow is best known for his Hierachy of Needs. A hierarchy is a list of things in some sort of order – for example, important things at the top and less important things at the bottom. Maslow believed that inside every human being there are five needs. We can put them into a pyramid. Look at Figure 1 on your handout. At the base of the pyramid are the physiological needs – the needs for food, drink and a place to sleep. At the next level there are the safety needs. Above safety needs are social needs. These include the need for love and friendship. Next there is the need for esteem. People need to develop self-respect and to feel that other people respect them, too. At the top of the pyramid is an even more complicated idea. Maslow called it Self-Actualisation. Put simply, this means achieving everything that you are capable of achieving. Not many people reach that level. This is why he has drawn the hierarchy as a pyramid.
Maslow's key point about the hierarchy is this: a person is not motivated by higher level needs until the lower level needs have been satisfied. In other words, a person is not motivated by concerns for safety if he is hungry or thirsty. But once that need for food and drink is satisfied, it no longer motivates. Now, a person can only be motivated by greater safety in his life. And so on.

Presenter: **G Listen to the third part of the lecture. Make notes on the life of Herzberg.**
Female lecturer: OK. So that's Abraham Maslow. The second writer I want to talk about today is Frederick Herzberg, that's H-E-R-Z-B-E-R-G. Herzberg was a psychologist. He

was born on April 18th, 1923, in the United States. His parents were poor, like Maslow's, and, like Maslow's, they were immigrants, from Lithuania, which in the 1920s was part of Russia. Herzberg did very well at school and, when he was 16, he won a place at college. While he was there, he got married, in 1944. He got his BS in 1946, his MS in Industrial Psychology in 1949 and his PhD the following year. He worked as a manager of a research laboratory from 1951 to 1957, and then became a professor of psychology at a university in Ohio. Herzberg wrote several books, including *Motivation to Work* in 1959. In this book, he described his famous theory of satisfiers and dissatisfiers. He died on January 19th, 2000.

Presenter: **H 1 Look at Figure 1 again. Listen to the fourth part. Label each item in the figure either Hygiene factor (H) or Motivator (M).**

Female lecturer: Herzberg knew about the work of Maslow, of course, but he developed a theory with a very important difference. Let's compare Herzberg's ideas with Maslow's. Look at Figure 1 again. Herzberg said Maslow's lower-level needs – physiological and safety – are not motivators. He called them 'hygiene' factors. Hygiene means keeping things clean. We teach children hygiene when we say, 'Wash your hands before you eat a meal. Clean your teeth after your meal.' Hygiene helps to prevent disease. In the same way, Herzberg said, a good salary and a safe place to work are just hygiene factors. They prevent workers being dissatisfied, but they don't motivate them. According to Herzberg, the motivators are the higher-level needs of Maslow's hierarchy – esteem and self-actualisation. These are the things that make people work harder.

Presenter: **I Listen to the fifth part.**

Female lecturer: What does Herzberg's theory mean for managers? It means they must make sure all the hygiene factors are in place, but they must also make sure that employees are valued as people. There's quite a good story about this. A man sees three people working on a building site. He says to the first man, 'What are you doing?' The man says, 'I don't know. I just work here.' He asks the second man. He says, 'I'm cutting these stones so they are perfectly straight, and then I'm putting them on top of each other to make a perfect wall.' And he says to the third man, 'What are you doing?' And the third man says, 'I'm helping to build this mosque.' What does that story tell us? The first man is not motivated to work hard. The second man is working hard, perhaps, but for his own satisfaction. He doesn't see how his work fits into the whole job. The third man knows how important his job is. He is motivated because he sees the value of his work.
OK. We've run out of time. More next week …

Presenter: **Theme 4: Science and Nature, Tornadoes and Hurricanes**
Lesson 1: Vocabulary
A 2 Listen and check your answers.

Voice: The Sahara Desert occupies a third of the African continent.
In fact, it occupies around eight per cent of the land area of the Earth.
In total, it is about eight million square kilometres.
It is expanding at the rate of about one kilometre a month.

But the Sahara is not just sand. In fact, there are about 1,000 different types of plant.

Presenter: **B 2 Listen and check your ideas.**
Voice: The *haboob* is a turning sandstorm or duststorm. Its name comes from the Arabic word for strong wind. It can reach up to two kilometres wide and one kilometre high. It travels across the land at speeds of between 50 and 80 kilometres per hour. A *haboob* can last from one hour up to three hours. The *haboob* occurs mainly in the Sahara, but can also appear in the southwestern states of the United States. How does a *haboob* form? Air falls from thunderclouds in their final stage. When the falling air hits the ground, it picks up huge amounts of sand or dust. The wall of sand moves forward with the thunderclouds.

Presenter: **Lesson 2: Listening**
D Listen to the first part of the talk.
Roger Dawkins: Today I'm going to talk about tornadoes. Firstly, I'm going to define a tornado. Secondly, I'm going to talk about the origins of the word. Then I'll tell you about the size, speed and duration of tornadoes. Next, I'll explain where they occur and when. After that, I'll describe two scales for measuring tornadoes. Finally, I'm going to talk about three theories that try to explain why tornadoes form.

Presenter: **E Listen to the second part of the talk.**
Roger Dawkins: So, first, what is a tornado? A tornado is a column of wind which is turning violently. The name comes from a Spanish word meaning 'thunderstorm'. The average tornado is 100 metres across – that's about the length of a football field – and it turns at 500 kilometres per hour – that's about four times as fast as the speed limit on a motorway. However, the magnitude and turning speed can vary enormously. Tornadoes *can* reach one kilometre across – that's 10 football pitches – and can turn at 800 kilometres per hour – that's the speed of a commercial aeroplane. By the way, don't confuse the *turning* speed with the *travelling* speed, that is the speed across the ground. Tornadoes travel quickly, but not at 500 kilometres an hour. They move across the land at about 50 kilometres an hour, although they can go two or three times that speed. I don't know if you saw that film of people trying to outrun a tornado in their car. They were filming a tornado in the distance when, suddenly, they realised that it was coming in their direction. It was very frightening, because the tornado caught up with them, even though they were driving very fast, but they kept filming out of the back of the vehicle, right up to the moment when they crashed the car. Nobody was hurt, thankfully.
Anyway, where was I? Oh, yes, size and speed can vary enormously. Similarly, the duration of tornadoes covers a wide range. Most only last a few minutes, but some go on for up to two hours.
Lastly, the distance they travel. Again, there's a big range – from about seven kilometres to over 200. Incidentally, some tornadoes can cause some very strange effects. Tornadoes do not contain rain, but things can fall out of the sky after a tornado. For example, a recent story comes from the town of Villa Angel Flores in Mexico. At 11 p.m. on June 2nd, 1997, small creatures began to fall on the town. They were toads – a kind of frog. The explanation came

eventually. A tornado picked up the toads from a lake and dropped them several kilometres away on the town. So, if you hear an English person say, 'It's raining cats and dogs', he or she might be telling the truth! Actually, that's got nothing to do with tornadoes. Cats and dogs used to sleep on the roofs of houses, and when the roofs got very wet from heavy rain, they fell off … so people said, 'It's raining cats and dogs.'

OK, so tornadoes are columns of turning wind. Now let's see where they happen. Well, turning winds occur all over the world, but tornadoes are the most violent kind, and the destructive ones occur mostly in the United States. In fact, most of them happen in just one part of the United States, in an area of the central plains called Tornado Alley. The US experiences more than 500 tornadoes every year. There are also tornadoes in Western Europe, India, China, Japan and Australia.

OK. We've heard that tornadoes occur in many parts of the world. But when do they occur? Summer or winter? Daytime or night-time? Morning or evening? Tornadoes can occur at any time of the day, in any month of the year. In the United States, however, three-quarters of tornadoes arise from March to July, with the majority in May.

Now let's consider how we can measure tornadoes. We can measure tornadoes on two main scales, the Fujita scale – that's F-U-J-I-T-A – and the Torro scale – T-O-R-R-O. Both scales classify the speed and destructive power of the tornado. The Fujita scale goes from 0 to 5, whereas the Torro scale runs from 0 to 12. On the Torro scale, one is mild; the wind will blow down small trees and blow off the tops of chimneys. Twelve is a super-tornado; the wind will move cars over 100 metres and even steel-reinforced buildings will be seriously damaged.

Presenter: **G 2 Listen to the third part of the talk.**

Roger Dawkins:

So now we know what tornadoes are and where they occur. We also know how to measure them. But how do tornadoes form? There are three theories about this.

The first theory is the main one. It's called the Rising Air Theory. This theory says that tornadoes happen when a long column of quickly rising air stretches up from the ground. It often goes to a thundercloud. This can happen when the ground gets very hot and a bubble of air starts rising.

Now let's consider the second theory. The second theory is called the Downward Spiral Theory. This suggests that the tornado develops in a downward direction from a thunderstorm cloud to the ground.

Finally, the third theory. This is the Electrical Storm Theory. I'm going to tell you a story to explain this theory. One day, in the middle of a storm, a farmer looked up into the heart of a tornado. What could he see? The farmer said the middle of the tornado was constantly lit by lightning flashes. So the Electrical Storm Theory says that lightning is the cause of tornadoes.

So, to sum up, we don't really know the exact cause of tornadoes. It could be rising air, a downward spiral or lightning.

That's all for this week. In next week's programme, we'll look at another violent turning wind – the hurricane.

Presenter: **Lesson 4: Applying new skills**

A 3 Listen and check your ideas.

Voice:
tornado
kilometres
violent
incidentally
electrical
develop
classify
damaged
seriously
destructive
vary
effects

Presenter: **C Listen to the first part of the talk.**

Roger Dawkins:

Welcome to *Violent Nature*. Last week, I talked about tornadoes. This week, I'm going to talk about another powerful turning wind – the hurricane. Firstly, I'm going to explain what a hurricane is and tell you the origins of the name. Secondly, I'm going to tell you where and when they occur. Next, I'll describe some ways of measuring hurricanes. Finally, I'm going to talk about two theories that try to explain how hurricanes form.

Presenter: **D Listen to the second part of the talk.**

Roger Dawkins:

So, first, what is a hurricane? Well, it's a turning wind, like a tornado, but there are two main differences between hurricanes and tornadoes. Firstly, hurricanes only start over water, whereas tornadoes only start over land. Secondly, hurricanes are huge rainstorms, whereas tornadoes don't have any rain in them.

I suppose you could add a third difference. Hurricanes are much more destructive than tornadoes. In fact, hurricanes are the most destructive form of weather in the world. A hurricane that hit the American city of Galveston in 1900 is still considered to be the worst natural disaster in US history. More than 37,000 people died and 3,600 buildings were completely destroyed.

Now there is more protection for people and buildings against hurricanes, but Hurricane Andrew, which hit the US in 1993, still killed 26 people and caused over 25 billion dollars worth of damage.

By the way, perhaps you have noticed that hurricanes always have the names of people – like Andrew. This practice started in Australia in the early 1900s. An Australian called Clement Wragge introduced the idea. It is said that he gave each hurricane the name of a person that he didn't like. Nowadays, a committee decides on the list of names for hurricanes. You can find the list of names for the next few years on www.fema.gov/kids/hunames.htm. That's www dot f-e-m-a dot g-o-v forward slash kids forward slash h-u-n-a-m-e-s dot h-t-m.

Anyway, the name *hurricane* itself comes from Mayan – M-A-Y-A-N – the language of the tribes who lived in Mexico hundreds of years ago. Hurakan, spelt H-U-R-A-K-A-N was a god who breathed on the oceans and made dry land. Later, Indians who lived in the Caribbean used the name Hurican – H-U-R-I-C-A-N – as the name of an evil god, and many years later the University of Miami adopted the name, with a change in spelling, for any strong turning storm, that forms over warm water with winds above 119 kilometres an hour.

OK, so hurricanes, like tornadoes, are turning storms. Now, let's see where they happen. Well, as I said just now, hurricanes form over warm water, so we don't get hurricanes in the Antarctic Ocean. In fact, the temperature of the air above the water must be more than 27 degrees centigrade, so the majority of hurricanes form in the tropics. In fact, there are six main areas, including the Western Atlantic, the Eastern Pacific and the South Indian oceans. Incidentally, you can see where the current hurricanes are all over the world if you go to www.solar.ifa.hawaii.edu. That's w-w-w dot s-o-l-a-r dot i-f-a dot hawaii dot e-d-u.

OK. So we've seen that hurricanes occur in many parts of the world. But when do they happen? Is there a hurricane season, in the same way as there is a tornado season? Well, the answer is 'yes and no'. Hurricanes generally happen in the summer, but the length of the hurricane season varies in each hurricane area. For example, the Atlantic hurricane season officially starts on June 1 and ends on November 30, but most tropical storms and hurricanes form between August 15 and October 15. By contrast, hurricanes occur year-round in the western North Pacific, while in the North Indian Ocean, there are two peaks of activity, in May and November.

Now let's consider how we can measure hurricanes. The most commonly used scale is the Saffir-Simpson scale. The scale runs from 1 to 5, with a Level 1 hurricane having winds of 119 to 153 kilometres per hour. This level causes minimal damage, mainly to trees and bushes. Level 5, on the other hand, has wind speeds of up to 270 kilometres an hour and causes catastrophic damage to buildings and great loss of life. By the way, don't be confused by the numbers on the Saffir-Simpson scale. A Level 5 hurricane is not five times as violent as a Level 1 hurricane. It's not even 50 times as violent. It is 500 times as violent.

Presenter: **G Listen to the talk again. Check your answers to the questions in Exercise F.**
[REPEAT OF LESSON 4, EXERCISE D]

Presenter: **H Listen to the final part of the talk. Draw a diagram showing the formation of hurricanes according to each theory.**

Roger Dawkins:
So now we know what hurricanes are and where they occur. We also know how to measure them. But how do hurricanes form? There are two theories about this.

The first theory is the main one. It's called the Convection Theory. Convection, which is spelt C-O-N-V-E-C-T-I-O-N, means air moving upwards. Air starts to turn slowly over a tropical ocean. Hot air inside rises. More air is sucked in at the bottom and that air rises, too. The air on the outside starts to turn more quickly. This process continues and grows until a hurricane is formed. The hurricane continues to grow until it moves over land or over cooler water. Now let's consider the second theory. It is called the Electromagnetic Theory. Some scientists believe that hurricanes occur when the Earth gets closer to the sun. This happens from June to November every year. According to this theory, the sun has an influence on part of the Earth's atmosphere, which causes areas of low pressure. These areas produce clouds and electrical storms. The electrical activity starts a turning wind and, eventually, a hurricane forms. So, to sum up, most people believe that hurricanes

form when more and more air is sucked up in organised convection, but some people believe electrical activity is the cause.

That's all for this week. Next week, we are going to look at some more forces of nature – not weather this time, but movements that start inside the Earth itself.

Presenter: **Theme 5: The Physical World, Natural Disasters**
Lesson 1: Vocabulary
B Listen and look at the pictures. Copy the green words and phrases into one or both columns.

Voice:
There are many similarities between earthquakes and volcanoes. Both can cause natural disasters. When an earthquake occurs in a town or city, the earth shakes violently, and this can cause a lot of damage to buildings. This often leads to many deaths. In a similar way, when a volcano erupts near a town or city, the hot rocks and ash can damage buildings and kill people. Both kinds of event can also cause tidal waves. In fact, tidal waves after earthquakes or volcanic eruptions often cause more damage than the original event.

There are also some differences between earthquakes and volcanoes. Earthquakes usually only last for a few seconds or minutes, whereas volcanoes can erupt for days or even months. With a volcano, fire often shoots high into the air, while earthquakes are not usually linked with fire from underground. Of course, damaged buildings often catch fire after an earthquake.

Presenter: **Lesson 2: Listening**
A Listen to the introduction. What exactly are you going to hear about in this lecture?

Female lecturer:
There are two natural disasters that have killed millions of people in the history of the Earth. One shakes the ground, the other explodes and sends rocks and fire out of the ground. We call the first one an earthquake. We call the second one a volcano. For centuries, people believed there was a relationship between earthquakes and volcanoes. Do earthquakes cause volcanoes? Do volcanoes cause earthquakes? Or does something else cause both of them? This week, we are going to look at earthquakes, next week we will look at volcanoes, and by the end of the two lectures you should be able to answer the question: *What is the relationship between these two terrible natural disasters?*

So this week we are going to hear about early theories of the cause of earthquakes, and then we are going to hear about a famous earthquake that led to scientific research in Europe. We are then going to hear how the real cause of earthquakes was finally discovered.

Presenter: **C Listen to the first part of the lecture.**

Female lecturer:
Thousands of years ago, people believed that there were huge animals that lived underground. Some people thought they were snakes, others believed they were turtles. Some even said they were giant spiders. According to these people, the animals sometimes got angry and when they did, the earth shook. Aristotle, the famous Greek philosopher of the 4th century B.C.E., did not believe in giant underground animals. His explanation was almost as strange, though. He thought there were huge winds under the earth that sometimes caused the ground to shake. In fact, the Greek word for 'shaking' is

seismos – S-E-I-S-M-O-S. Eventually, therefore, the science of earthquakes became known as *seismology*.

Presenter: **D Listen to the second part of the lecture.**

Female lecturer: The earliest recorded earthquake was in 1177 B.C.E. in China, but scientists in Europe were not interested in earthquakes until around 1750 C.E. At that time, earthquakes started to shake England. This was very unusual, and the English scientists of the day became interested in them. These small earthquakes were warnings of a much bigger earthquake. On Sunday November 1st, 1755, a huge earthquake hit the city of Lisbon, in Portugal. The earthquake, and the tidal wave that followed it, flattened the city and killed around 70,000 people. There were eyewitness accounts of the terrible scenes. One wrote:
We began to hear a rumbling noise, like that of carriages, which increased to such a degree as to equal the noise of the loudest cannon; and immediately we felt the first shock, which was succeeded by a second and a third; on which, as on the fourth, I saw several light flames of fire issuing from the sides of the mountains, resembling that which may be observed on the kindling of coal. . . . I observed from one of the hills called the Fojo that there issued a great quantity of smoke, very thick, but not very black which still increased with the fourth shock, and after continued to issue in a greater or less degree. Just as we heard the underground rumblings, we observed it would burst forth at the Fojo; for the quantity of smoke was always proportional to the underground noise.
Anyway, after the Lisbon earthquake, scientists in Europe realised that earthquakes could be very dangerous, and they began to record the times and locations of earthquakes. They also began to work on ways of measuring earthquakes. As communications between countries got better, scientists in Europe began to collect observations from places as far away as South America and Japan. In the early 19th century, scientists suspected that there was something about the geology or type of rock in particular places that led to earthquakes.

Presenter: **E 2 Listen to the third part and check your ideas.**

Female ecturer: In the 1850s, the first true seismologist appeared, a man called Robert Mallet, and in 1880 the first instrument for measuring earthquakes was invented, by a man called John Milne, while he was working in Japan. He called it a seismograph.
In the United States, a man called Gilbert studied the rocks after an earthquake and decided that the lines he found in the rocks came before the earthquake, not after it. These lines were called faults. Similarly, a man called Reid studied fault lines in rocks after the 1906 San Francisco earthquake. He concluded that pressure builds up along a fault line and is eventually released as an earthquake.

Presenter: **F 2 Listen to the fourth part and check your ideas.**

Female lecturer: What is a fault line? How does it occur? If you look at a map showing the main earthquake areas, you can see immediately that earthquakes are more common in some places than others. Why is this? In the 1920s, a German meteorologist and astronomer named Alfred Wegener proposed a startling theory. He said the continents were not fixed in their

position on the globe. Instead, they were moving around on huge plates. In some places, the plates come together. This is where earthquakes happen. At first, other scientists laughed at his ideas, but gradually, people found more and more evidence for his plate theory.

Presenter: **G Listen to the fifth part and draw a diagram from the information.**

Female lecturer: We now know that Reid's conclusion about earthquakes and fault lines is correct. The main cause of earthquakes is the movement of the rocks along fault lines where two continental plates meet. One plate is trying to move north, for example. The other plate is trying to move south. Friction between the rocks on each plate prevents this from happening. Pressure builds up, until finally, the rocks slide against each other. We call this an earthquake. There are more than 100 earthquakes a day. Incidentally, if you want to see the location of current earthquakes, go to www.gps.caltech.edu and follow the links to earthquakes and records of the day.
How do the plates move? Actually, the solid rock that we see on the surface of the Earth is lying on a layer of very soft rock. The plates can slide on this soft rock. Very, very slowly, but they can slide.
So, in a strange way, Aristotle was almost right about earthquakes. There are no winds under the ground to move the rocks around, but there is a kind of river that is moving all the time – a river of soft rock.

Presenter: **Lesson 3: Learning new skills**
A 3 Listen and check your ideas.

Voice: a Some people thought they were snakes, others believed they were turtles. Some even said they were giant spiders.
b Aristotle thought there were huge winds under the earth that sometimes caused the ground to shake.
c After the Lisbon earthquake, scientists in Europe realised that earthquakes could be very dangerous.
d In the early 19th century, scientists suspected that there was something about the geology in particular places that led to earthquakes.
e Gilbert decided that fault lines in rocks came *before* the earthquake, not after it.
f Reid concluded that pressure builds up along a fault line and is eventually released as an earthquake.
g Wegener proposed a startling theory.

Presenter: **C 1 Listen to the first signposts from the lecture in Lesson 2. Can you remember how the lecturer continues in each case?**

Female lecturer: 1 One plate is trying to move north, for example.
2 Some people thought there were snakes underground.
3 The continents were not fixed in their position on the globe.
4 At first, other scientists laughed at Wegener's ideas, …

Presenter: **2 Listen and check your ideas.**

Female lecturer: 1 One plate is trying to move north, for example. The other plate is trying to move south.
2 Some people thought there were snakes underground. Other people believed there were turtles.

3 The continents were not fixed in their position on the globe. Instead, they were moving around on huge plates.

4 At first, other scientists laughed at Wegener's ideas, but gradually people found more and more evidence for his plate theory.

Presenter: **3 Listen to some more first signposts. What will come next?**

Voice:
1 On the one hand, I want to go out this evening.
2 One parent wants his son to be a doctor.
3 Some people like meat.
4 I did not wait for the person to call me.
5 At first, nobody believed him, …

Presenter: **Lesson 4: Applying new skills**
A 3 Listen and check your ideas.

Voice:
natural
disaster
explodes
earthquake
volcano
observations
communications
geology
eventually
evidence
concluded
meteorologist

Presenter: **C Listen to the introduction.**

Female lecturer:
Last week we looked at earthquakes and we saw that they are caused by the movement of the continental plates. This week, we are going to look at another natural disaster, volcanoes. We are going to consider a number of questions. What is the origin of the name? When and where was the most famous volcanic eruption? Why is it famous? How do volcanoes appear? How long do they take to form? And finally, what is the relationship between earthquakes and volcanoes?

Presenter: **D Listen to the first part of the lecture.**

Female lecturer:
The word 'volcano' comes from the name of a small island in the Mediterranean Sea. Hundreds of years ago, people living in the area noticed fire coming out of the mountain on the island. They believed that the mountain was the chimney of a blacksmith's shop owned by a man called Vulcan. A blacksmith is a person who works with hot metal to make shoes for horses and metal objects like swords. According to legend, Vulcan the blacksmith made weapons for Mars, the Roman god of war. So, some people believed volcanoes were the flames from underground fires. Others thought there was fire under the whole of the Earth. Aristotle, as we have heard, said there were winds rushing around under the Earth. These winds caused earthquakes and, when they broke through the Earth, they caused volcanoes.

Presenter: **E 3 Listen to the second part and check or complete the table.**

Female lecturer:
What is the most famous volcanic eruption? Well, you have probably heard of it. It occurred in Italy in 79 C.E. On that day, the volcano Vesuvius erupted. It destroyed several places, including the city of Pompeii. But why is the eruption so famous? Firstly, the event was described by Pliny the Younger in two

letters. In his eyewitness account he wrote:
The cloud was rising from Vesuvius. I can best describe its shape by likening it to a pine tree. It rose into the sky on a very long 'trunk' from which spread some 'branches.' Some parts of the cloud were white; other parts were dark with dirt and ash ….
Meanwhile, broad sheets of flame were lighting up many parts of Vesuvius; their light and brightness were the more vivid for the darkness of the night. The buildings were being rocked by a series of strong tremors, and appeared to have come loose from their foundations and to be sliding this way and that. Outside, however, there was danger from the rocks that were coming down …
As the column of ash rose over 30 kilometres, and over 3,000 people died, Pliny watched and wrote his account of the eruption.

However, Pliny's eyewitness account was not enough to ensure that Pompeii went down in history. In fact, the story of the eruption was completely forgotten over the years, and Pompeii lay buried under metres of ash. Then, the city was rediscovered. A small amount of excavation happened in the early 1800s, then, in 1860, an archaeologist called Giuseppe Fiorelli – that's F-I-O-R-E-L-L-I, became director of the excavations. Fiorelli realised that the bodies under the ash had completely disappeared but had left empty spaces. He poured plaster into the empty spaces, then dug away the ash. We can still see the result of his work today. One is a dog trying to get free from its chain at the moment of death. Another is a young man trying to protect an old woman from the falling ash.

Incidentally, the eruption of Vesuvius is certainly not the earliest recorded volcanic eruption. Before the time of written language, someone painted a picture on the wall of a house in Catal Hayuk in modern-day Turkey. It shows a volcano erupting. Archaeologists have dated the painting to about 6200 BCE.

Presenter: **F Listen to the third part of the lecture. Draw a diagram to show the modern theory of volcano formation.**

Female lecturer:
Anyway, where was I? Oh, yes. How do volcanoes appear? As we heard last week, scientists believe that there is a layer of soft rock under the hard rock at the surface of the Earth. The hard rock is moving around on the soft rock on huge continental plates. When the pressure builds at the meeting point of two plates, earthquakes occur. However, sometimes, when two plates meet, one plate is forced under the other plate. The plates rub together and friction turns the rock to a liquid called magma, spelt M-A-G-M-A. The plates continue to move and the pressure increases. Finally, the magma is forced to the surface and erupts out of the ground as a volcano.

Presenter: **G Listen to the fourth part of the lecture. Make notes of the important information.**

Female lecturer:
How long does it take volcanoes to form? Most volcanoes form over millions of years. Some, however, appear and grow very quickly. I don't know if you have heard about the volcano that appeared in Mexico in 1943. A farmer in a place called Paricutin looked out of his window one day and saw that his donkey was standing on a small hill. This was strange, because the night before he tied the donkey to a tree in a flat field. He went and untied the donkey before the rope strangled him. Then he

watched in amazement as the hill grew and grew. Another farmer, Domini Pulido explained how the eruptions started:

In the afternoon I heard a noise, like thunder during a rainstorm. At 4 p.m., I noticed that a small hole had opened in the ground. Then the ground raised itself two metres high, and a kind of smoke or fine dust – grey, like ashes – began to rise up. Immediately more smoke began to rise, with a hiss or whistle, loud and continuous, and there was a smell of sulphur. I then became greatly frightened.

Anyway, the volcano at Paricutin grew to a height of 336 metres in the next year and began erupting the day after it first appeared. Eruptions continued for eight years and lava spread over an area of 25 square kilometres. By the way, lava is the name we give to the magma or liquid rock when it flows out of the volcano.

So, the volcano at Paricutin grew in just eight years. Similarly, a volcano grew in the sea near Iceland in just four years. In fact, the volcano grew 130 metres from the seabed to the surface in just six months, from May to November 1963. At first, there were no eruptions. Then the volcano appeared above the surface, and it began to erupt. The lava eventually created a new island of three square kilometres and 170 metres at its highest point. Local people called the volcanic island Surtsey, after a fire giant in Icelandic stories.

Presenter: **H 2 Listen and check your ideas.**

Female lecturer: OK. So to sum up. Do earthquakes cause volcanoes? Do volcanoes cause earthquakes? No. Earthquakes do not cause volcanoes and volcanoes do not cause earthquakes. Instead, both earthquakes and volcanoes are caused by the movement of the continental plates. Incidentally, there are more than 1,500 active volcanoes in the world at the moment. You can see the latest information about eruptions if you go to http://volcano.und.nodak.edu – that's h-t-t-p://v-o-l-c-a-n-o dot u-n-d dot n-o-d-a-k dot e-d-u – and follow the links to current eruptions. OK. Next week, we are going to talk about other natural disasters, like tidal waves and floods, and find out the cause of each.

Presenter: **Theme 6: Culture and Civilization, What Is Society?**
Lesson 1: Vocabulary
B Read and listen to this introduction to a lecture. Then complete the text with one of the green words in each space.

Male lecturer: We talk a lot nowadays about society and culture and civilization. We even have a new branch of education – sociology – which is the study of society. But have you ever stopped to ask yourself: What is society? What is culture? What is civilization? What is the relationship between the three words? According to the dictionary, society is the organisation of individuals into social groups. Culture, on the other hand, is defined as the customs and achievements of a society. Individuals organise into social groups that become a society. The society then develops customs and achieves certain things. This makes the society into a culture. What about a civilization? Again, the dictionary helps. A civilization is a culture that has achieved important advances in science and art.

Presenter: **D 2 Listen to these stressed syllables. Number the green words in the order you hear the stressed syllables.**

Voice : 1 chie
2 ci
3 cul
4 la
5 ol
6 van
7 vid
8 so

Presenter: **Lesson 2: Listening**
A 2 Listen to the introduction. Make notes. Check your answers to Exercise 1.

Male lecturer: We talk a lot nowadays about society and culture and civilization. We even have a new branch of education – sociology – which is the study of society. But have you ever stopped to ask yourself: What is society? What is culture? What is civilization? What is the relationship between the three words? In this talk, I am going to consider these questions and several other questions that are related to them. Is it natural for people to form into social groups? Is society more important than individuals, or are individuals more important than society? What are the common features of a society? Next week, we will look at some other points about society and culture.

Presenter: **B Listen to the first part of the lecture.**

Male lecturer: So, first, what is society and what is [PAUSE] culture? According to the [PAUSE] dictionary, society is the organisation of individuals into [PAUSE] groups. Culture, on the other [PAUSE] hand, is defined as the customs and achievements of a [PAUSE] society. Individuals organise into social [PAUSE] groups that become a society. The society then develops customs and achieves certain [PAUSE] things. This makes the society into a [PAUSE] culture. What about a [PAUSE] civilization? Again, the dictionary [PAUSE] helps. A civilization is a culture that has achieved important [PAUSE] advances in science and [PAUSE] art. So the relationship is – society forms a [PAUSE] culture that, sometimes, becomes a [PAUSE] civilization.

Presenter: **C 3 Listen to the second part of the lecture. Make notes.**

Male lecturer: The next question is: Is it natural for people to form into social groups? Many people believe that it is. The great Arab scholar, Ibn Khaldoun, wrote extensively about society in his book *Muqaddimah*. Ibn Khaldoun was born in Tunis in 1332. Incidentally, the Khalduniyah area in Tunis has hardly changed since his day, and one can still see the house in which, according to tradition, he was born. Anyway, Ibn Khaldoun's father was an important man, but in 1348, when Ibn Khaldoun was only 16, a terrible disease called the Black Death came to Tunis and killed both his parents. I don't know if you know that the Black Death was one of the biggest dangers of the 14th century. It killed over 25 million people in Europe in just five years. Anyway, where was I? Oh, yes. The death of his parents had a deep effect on Ibn Khaldoun, as we shall see later. When he was only 20, Ibn Khaldoun served at the court in Tunis and then went abroad to Morocco and Spain to represent his country. Finally, in 1375, he retired from politics and went to live with the tribe of Awlad 'Arif, in present-day Algeria. For the next four years, he concentrated on writing his *Universal History, Kitab al-Ibar*, of which the massive introduction, the *Muqaddimah*, is the most important section. In fact, his writings are so important that some people called him the father of sociology. Ibn Khaldoun believed in the idea of '*asabiyah*, which can be translated as 'social cohesion' or joining together. He said that this cohesion appears naturally in tribes and other small social groups. He went on to claim that the social cohesion will be stronger if the society develops a strong religion. Ibn Khaldoun thought that social cohesion is the driving force of society, the thing that pushes the civilization forwards and makes it strong. When the cohesion weakens, for any reason, the society weakens and another society with a stronger cohesion takes its place. Ibn Khaldoun died in Cairo in 1406.

Presenter:	**E**	**3 Listen to the third part of the lecture. Number the features in the green box in order.**
Male lecturer:		But what exactly is a society or a culture? How can we recognise a cultural group?

If we bring together the ideas of various sociologists, we can identify at least 10 features that societies have in common.

1 There are particular laws. For example, in the UK you are not allowed to marry until you are 16 years old, and only then with your parents' consent.

2 There are particular standards – things that people normally do. These are called 'social norms'. *Norm* comes from the word *normal*. Again, in the UK, people usually give up their seats to disabled people on a bus or train. This is a social norm.

3 People in the society trade with each other. In other words, they buy and sell things or, in a primitive society, they exchange things. For example, in old farming societies, one person might make bread and exchange it with another person for vegetables, whereas in more sophisticated societies, people form companies and the companies trade with each other.

4 People use technology to change the natural world. At its simplest, the society makes tools to help cultivate crops. In a more advanced example, scientists may make rain by spraying the clouds with chemicals.

5 People know the correct language to use in different situations. For example, in many cultures there is, on the one hand, an informal variety of the language for social contact, and on the other a formal variety of the language for business. In some countries, two completely different languages are used for social and business contact. I don't know if you know that in Finland a person will socialise in Finnish but conduct business in English.

6 People educate their children. The form of education depends on the society. Perhaps the men educate the young boys and the women educate the young girls, or perhaps the society has a formal system of schooling, from primary through secondary to college or university.

7 People have time for leisure. In other words, they are not working every hour of the day. They may spend the time on sports or on producing artistic work, but they are not struggling to survive from day to day.

8 There are traditional stories, superstitions, folk tales, songs and myths. For example, the Greeks had *Aesop's Fables*, or stories, the Arab World had *The Thousand and One Nights*.

9 There is traditional food and methods of cooking. This is so important that societies are sometimes named from their food. English people call French people 'frogs' because some French people eat frogs' legs. In turn, French people used to call English people *le rote boeuf*, or the roast beef, because they ate roast beef. Anyway, the point is that traditional food and methods of cooking are very important to a cultural group.

10 The society marks 'rites of passage' in particular ways. Rites of passage are the special events of people's lives – birth, coming of age, marriage and death. People are often shocked by the rites of passage in a different culture. Did you know that there was a tradition at one time in India that the widow of a dead man must burn herself on his funeral fire? Many people outside the culture found this shocking, and the British tried to stop it when they ruled India.

Presenter:	**Lesson 3: Learning new skills** **A 2 Listen and check your ideas.**
Voice:	a According to the dictionary, society is the organisation of individuals into groups.
	b Culture, on the other hand, is defined as the customs and achievements of a society.
	c Incidentally, the Khalduniyah area in Tunis has hardly changed since his day.
	d The death of his parents had a deep effect on Ibn Khaldoun, as we shall see later.
	e That's about a third of the population at the time. Imagine that. One in three people died.
	f The form of education depends on the society.
	g People have time for leisure. In other words, they are not working every hour of the day.
	h English people call French people 'frogs' because some French people eat frogs' legs. In turn, French people used to call English people *le rote boeuf*, or the roast beef, because they ate roast beef.
	i The point is that traditional food and methods of cooking are very important to a cultural group.

Presenter:	**B 3 Listen to a section of the lecture again. How does the lecturer show that Sentences B are Ibn Khaldoun's opinion?** [REPEAT OF LESSON 2 EXERCISE C3]
Presenter:	**D Listen again to the last part of the lecture in Lesson 2. After each section, give an example from your own culture.** [REPEAT OF LESSON 2 EXERCISE E3]
Presenter:	**Lesson 4: Applying new skills** **B 2 Listen to the introduction and check your answers.**
Male lecturer:	Last week, I talked about society and culture. I listed the common features of societies or cultural groups. Today, I want to look at some more questions about society and look at the answers that various sociologists have come up with throughout history. These are the questions we are going to consider today.

Is society more important than individuals, or are individuals more important than society? Do all societies go through the same stages? Do we learn from history, or do we keep repeating the same mistakes?

Presenter: **C 2 Listen to the first part of the lecture.**

Male lecturer: OK. First question. Is society more important than individuals, or are individuals more important than society? This is one of the really big questions of sociology! In Ancient Greece, in the third and fourth centuries BCE, the philosophers Aristotle and Sophocles wrote about this question. They both believed that a person is only a real human being when he or she is part of society. Two thousand years later, in the late 19th century, the French sociologist Emile Durkheim agreed. He said that individuals depend on society for survival. Durkheim stated that people have a deep need to belong to something. Society helps them to fulfil that need. However, the German sociologist Max Weber, who was writing at the same time, did not agree with Durkheim. Instead, he thought that the individual is more important than society. He believed that the world only works when people act as individuals.

So, to sum up, we have two opposite views about individuals and society. Some philosophers and sociologists believe that individuals need society; some think that society needs individuals.

Presenter: **C 3 Listen again and complete the summary in the blue box.**
[REPEAT OF EXERCISE C2]

Presenter: **D 2 Listen to the second part of the lecture. Make notes of Ibn Khaldoun's opinions.**

Male lecturer: Our second question is this: Do all societies go through the same stages? Do you remember last time we talked about Ibn Khaldoun? He is the father of sociology, according to some people. Personally, I think that title is well-deserved. Anyway, he believed that all societies went through the same stages. His studies into the nature of society and social change led to the development of a new science, which he called 'ilm al-'umran, or the science of culture. He said all societies go through three stages. In the first stage they grow, in the second stage they produce advances in technology, in science and in art. In the final stage, they die. Sometimes they die because of internal influences – for example, the leaders of the society are not strong enough to hold the society together. Sometimes they die because of external influences, like a terrible disease. If you remember, Ibn Khaldoun's parents were killed by the Black Death, and I believe this event probably influenced his writings on this subject.

So, obviously, Ibn Khaldoun believed that history endlessly repeats itself, with societies in different times and different geographic locations showing the same changes in response to external events, such as the Black Death or foreign invasion, or internal developments, such as inventions or discoveries. No doubt he studied other civilizations and came to this rather sad conclusion. To put it another way, Ibn Khaldoun did not see any evidence of progress in individual cultures, except in the first stage, when they grow from a primitive to a civilized society.

Presenter: **E Listen to the second part again and identify them.**
[REPEAT OF EXERCISE D2]

Presenter: **F Listen to the third part of the lecture. Complete the statements in the bubbles.**

Male lecturer: So Ibn Khaldoun did not see any evidence of progress in individual cultures. Down the years, other thinkers have agreed with Ibn Khaldoun. The German philosopher Hegel, writing in the 18th century, said: 'The only thing we learn from history is that we *don't* learn from history.' He believed that we endlessly repeat the same mistakes. When society is faced with the same problem, according to Hegel, it reacts in the same way, even if that is not the best way to react. There is no actual improvement.

Many famous people throughout history have agreed with Ibn Khaldoun and Hegel. But one man, Marie-Jean de Caritat, did not agree. De Caritat was born in 1743 in France. He became a leading French philosopher and a strong supporter of education for everybody. He believed, quite simply, that mankind can continually improve and eventually become perfect. He imagined a future age in which there will be equality between nations and equality between people. He foresaw a future in which the individual will be perfect – morally, physically and intellectually. He was not just a dreamer. He accepted that people make mistakes and real progress is not easy for a culture. However, he believed that human beings can learn from their failures. He believed that there is no limit to human knowledge. He thought there is no end to human compassion for people who are ill or poor. He even claimed that human life can go on forever. He saw education for everybody as the key to this infinite improvement.

Two hundred years later, the British writer H.G. Wells saw the role of education in society in a rather more dramatic way. He said, 'Human history becomes more and more a race between education and disaster.' Wells believed in education. He obviously believed that there was a chance for education to save the world. But he was not sure that it would actually do so. What do you think? Do societies repeat the mistakes of earlier societies, or do we learn from history? Can education save us from ourselves?

Presenter: **Theme 7: They Made Our World, The Greatest Advance in History**
Lesson 1: Vocabulary
A 1 Listen and complete the diagram with a red word in each space.

Voice: There is a circle of progress that is repeated again and again in history. The circle works like this. Someone has a new idea. For example, an inventor sees someone dragging something heavy and thinks: 'He could move that more easily if he rolled it on a tree trunk.' This leads to a new invention – in this case, the wheel. Someone, perhaps the inventor, builds a new device from the invention – a wagon with wheels, for example, to carry goods, or a chariot for people to travel in. This device leads to a new technology, for example, wheeled transport. The new technology replaces the old technology. Suddenly, everything has wheels and people do not drag things across the ground any more. Then someone sees a horse pulling a wheeled cart and thinks: 'That cart would go much faster with an engine.'

Presenter: **B Listen to some information about a radio programme.**

Radio presenter: Last month on *They Made Our World*, we asked you to e-mail us with your list of the greatest advances of all time. We said it could be an invention or a discovery, but it must be something that revolutionised the world – something that changed the way we live or do something.

The response has been enormous – thousands of you have sent in your ideas already. But if you haven't e-mailed us yet, there is still time. Send your choice now to greatest at ourworld dotcom. Do it now and listen in at five o'clock today to find out the result. That's the greatest advance in the history of the world on *They Made Our World* on Channel 45 at five o'clock today.

Presenter: **C 2 Listen to the radio programme. Number the advances in order.**

Radio presenter: Welcome to They Made Our World. This week, we have the winner of our search to find the greatest advance in the history of the world. As you know, the response to our request for e-mails has been enormous, but we have a clear winner. I'm going to give you the top eight in reverse order. In other words, I'll give you number eight first, then number seven and so on, until we get to number one, our winner.

So, in eighth place we have … the telephone. I thought that would be higher, but there you are.

In seventh place, antibiotics. I never thought of those at all.

Sixth we have the printing press.

At number five we have mass production – I'm really surprised at that one.

Coming in at number four … food preservation. Apparently, you all think the world is a much better place for frozen chips and canned beans.

So now we have the top three. At number three, the internal combustion engine. You think it is important, but not as important as … at number two, the computer. I really thought that would be number one, but in fact, the top spot goes to the greatest advance in history … the wheel.

So there you have it. The wheel, the computer, the internal combustion engine, food preservation, mass production, the printing press, antibiotics and the telephone.

Presenter: **Lesson 2: Listening**
B Listen to Anne's talk straight through.

Female voice: What is the most important advance that people have made in the history of the world? Is it something to do with transport – the ability to move people and goods quickly around the world? Certainly, the Ancient World changed when the first Egyptian raised a piece of cloth as a sail and started to travel down the Nile. It is true that the wheel, for example, revolutionised transport and made it possible for one horse to move very heavy items over long distances. The invention of the internal combustion engine in the 19th century led to the conquest of the land, the sea and the air in the next 100 years. However, I do not believe the greatest advance in the history of the world has got anything to do with transport.

Is it something from the field of communications – the ability to send information quickly around the world? The Sumerians invented writing, which meant that information could be moved through time and space without people having to carry it in their heads. Johannes Gutenberg invented the printing press, which meant information could be copied and distributed all over the world quite cheaply. Telephones and then computers have led to the Communications Age, where everyone can talk or write to everyone else in the world instantly for a tiny amount of money. However, there is an advance that is much more important in the history of the world than anything from the field of communications.

I accept that advances in transport and communications were very important and, in a very real sense, the advances in these fields have made the modern world that we live in. But I believe there is a much more fundamental advance than either of these. I believe the greatest advance that human beings have made is in the area of food preservation. Let me explain. Man needs to eat food day in, day out. Early civilizations grew up near local sources of food. They needed large quantities of edible plants – fruit trees or nut trees, or bushes with berries. They needed herds of wild animals that they could kill and eat. However, there was a big problem with these natural supplies of food. On the one hand, in the correct season, usually the summer and autumn, the food was plentiful. But on the other hand, for large parts of the year, usually the winter months, there was little or no food. Why couldn't they store the food? Because, of course, most food goes bad very quickly if you just put it in a big storeroom.

For early societies, this was a serious problem. If you cannot store food, you must gather food every day, or at least every week. You must also kill animals regularly. This means that most people work from sunrise to sunset gathering food or hunting. There is very little time left for anything else – very little time for all the things we think of when we say civilization – science, the arts, industry, technology, leisure. The problem gets worse if the animals are wild and move from place to place. In this case, you must follow them when they move. So it is not possible to settle down in one place. And this is the essence of civilization. Civilization develops when settlements grow into towns, which in turn grow into large successful cities and then into empires. With food preservation comes civilization. The Ancient Egyptians knew how to dry fruit and corn to preserve it. The Inuit knew how to dry meat, and the Greeks and Romans salted food to keep it longer. The inhabitants of the Indus Valley pickled food to preserve it.

So this is what I believe. Before people discovered methods of preserving food, they spent all their time gathering food and hunting, often wandering from place to place following the animals they ate. Before food preservation existed, people could not settle down in one place and develop as a civilization. So food preservation is more important than anything to do with transport or communications or any other part of the modern world. Without food preservation, people would never have developed transport and communications anyway, because they would not have had the time or the settled communities to do it in.

OK, I hear you say. It was important in the old days to find a way of preserving food. But that problem was solved thousands of years ago. Not true. Throughout history, Man has struggled with the problem of preserving food. As we have seen, some progress was made with drying, salting and pickling thousands of years ago. But as soon as people moved away from a settled community, there were still great problems. Sailors often got a painful and potentially fatal disease called scurvy because they did not eat fresh fruit for months at a time. Scurvy struck the sailors on Magellan's journey around the world in 1519, for example. The same situation was repeated all over the world. Napoleon lost more men to scurvy and starvation in the war against Russia than he did in all the battles put together. In fact, the problem for Napoleon was so bad that the French government offered a reward of 12,000 francs to the person who could solve it. The result was … canning. A man called Nicholas Appert tried for years to win the prize. At first, he had no success, but gradually he solved the problem. Finally, he put food into airtight containers in an attempt to preserve it. It worked. So, by the 20th century, a lot of foodstuffs could be preserved, but fresh meat and dairy products were still a problem up to the 1950s. I remember my grandmother kept her meat in a small box called a meat safe. It was open to the air, but protected from flies by a mesh on the front. She kept her bottles of milk in the kitchen sink, floating in cold water. Of course, she had to use the milk the same day and the meat within two days, or it was bad. Nowadays, we can go to the supermarket once a week, buy fresh meat and dairy products and keep them in a freezer or a fridge. We can prepare a meal in a few moments and know that it is safe to eat. And what can we do with all the time we save? We can live.

So, in conclusion, food preservation first made it possible for a community as a whole to have time off from gathering, hunting and preparing food. With this time, civilizations invented the wheel and writing, the telephone and the computer. Without this time, no other inventions would have happened. More recently, food preservation has freed the housewife from the daily grind of food shopping and cooking. It is truly the greatest advance of all time.

Presenter: **C 2 Listen again and check your answers.**
[REPEAT OF LESSON 2 EXERCISE B]

Presenter: **Lesson 3: Learning new skills**
A 2 Listen and check your ideas.
Female
voice:
a Is it something to do with transport?
b Is it something in the field of communications?
c I accept that advances in transport and communications were very important and, in a very real sense, the advances in these fields have made the modern world that we live in.
d Sailors often got a painful and potentially fatal disease called scurvy because they did not eat fresh fruit for months at a time.
e It was important in the old days to find a way of preserving food.
f The Sumerians invented writing, which meant that information could be moved through time and space without people having to carry it in their heads.
g Johannes Gutenberg invented the printing press, which meant information could be copied and distributed all over the world quite cheaply.
h Man needs to eat food day in, day out.
i This means that most people work from sunrise to sunset gathering food or hunting.
j Before people discovered methods of preserving food, they spent all their time gathering food and hunting, often wandering from place to place following the animals that they ate.

k The problem gets worse if the animals are wild and move from place to place. In this case, you must follow them when they move.
l So it is not possible to settle down in one place.
m This is the essence of civilization.
n Civilization develops when settlements grow into towns, which in turn grow into large successful cities and then into empires.

Presenter: **Lesson 4: Applying new skills**
A 2 Listen again and check your ideas.
Female
voice:
OK, I hear you say. It was important in the old days to find a way of preserving food. But that problem was solved thousands of years ago. Not true. Throughout history, Man has struggled with the problem of preserving food. As we have seen, some progress was made with drying, salting and pickling thousands of years ago. But as soon as people moved away from a settled community, there were still great problems. Sailors often got a painful and potentially fatal disease called scurvy because they did not eat fresh fruit for months at a time. Scurvy struck the sailors on Magellan's journey around the world in 1519, for example. The same situation was repeated all over the world. Napoleon lost more men to scurvy and starvation in the war against Russia than he did in all the battles put together. In fact, the problem for Napoleon was so bad that the French government offered a reward of 12,000 francs to the person who could solve it. The result was canning. A man called Nicholas Appert tried for years to win the prize. At first, he had no success, but gradually he solved the problem. Finally, he put food into airtight bottles in an attempt to preserve it. It worked. So by the 20th century, a lot of foodstuffs could be preserved, but fresh meat and dairy products were still a problem up to the 1950s.

Presenter: **C Listen to the whole talk. Check your answers to Exercise B.**
Male voice:
What is the most important advance that people have made in the history of the world? Some might say it is mass production – the way that factories can produce huge quantities of goods nowadays with the help of machines, whereas in the past people had to make each item by hand. One definition of a civilization is a culture that changes the world in a clear way. Mass production has certainly enabled us to change the world out of all recognition. Most people (in the developed world at least) have a car, a television, a telephone and hundreds of other mass-produced items, things they could not have afforded if they were handmade. However, I think the greatest advance in the history of the world is more fundamental than material goods, like televisions and CD players.

What about computers? They are certainly a major part of nearly every area of modern-day life. With computers, we can calculate at an incredible speed and store and retrieve vast amounts of information. We can use them to play very sophisticated games or to store and reproduce hundreds of hours of music. Word-processing through computers has speeded up writing to an incredible extent. When I was young, I worked in an office, and we were expected to type up 10 perfect letters a day. Now we expect an office assistant to produce 50 or 60 letters a day, and then e-mail them to thousands of people at the same time, if necessary. But the invention of the modern computer comes at the end of a long trail of civilization. I believe the greatest advance comes a little earlier in our history.

I accept that mass production and computers have changed our world out of all recognition. Even my own grandfather would not understand most of the things I use in my everyday life, or the ways I use computers for work and pleasure. Computers make our lives more efficient, mass production gives us more things to own and enjoy. But, as I see it, neither computers nor mass production make our lives better in the most important way. In my opinion, the greatest advance that human beings have made is in the conquest of infectious diseases.

We have succeeded in conquering water-borne diseases like typhoid and cholera through better public health. Before people understood the need for clean water, decent housing and waste disposal, life for most people was short and full of pain. At the time of the Roman Empire, life expectancy in the civilized world was just 24 years. The Black Death in the 14th century killed a third of the population of the civilized world. Things had hardly improved by the start of the 20th century. In 1900, worldwide life expectancy was still only about 30 years. However, by 1985 it was about 62 years. This improvement is mainly due to better public health systems, but it is also due to the discovery of antibiotics and other powerful medicinal drugs.

Of course, you could argue that computers and mass production have made people's lives better. What is the point of having a long life if it is endless, hard, boring work?

I accept that this is true, but which is more important? To have a better life when you are well, or not to get an infectious disease in the first place? I maintain that first we had to give people lives free of pain and the fear of fatal illness. Then they could begin to enjoy their lives.

So, to sum up. I believe that the greatest advance in the history of the world is in the conquest of infectious diseases, through better public health and the discovery of powerful medicinal drugs to fight disease when it does occur. If you don't have a long life free from pain, you cannot enjoy the other advances of civilization.

Presenter: **Theme 8: Art and Literature, Gulliver and Robinson Crusoe**
Lesson 1: Vocabulary
A Listen to the past tense of the red words. Number the infinitives in order.

Voice:
1 let
2 saw
3 lit
4 needed
5 began
6 sold
7 belonged
8 landed
9 bought
10 disappeared
11 tricked
12 explored
13 heard
14 searched
15 thought
16 spent

Presenter: **C Listen to the introduction to the programme. Answer the questions.**

Female presenter:
Gulliver's Travels is one of the most famous books in English literature. In Swift's book, the hero, Lemuel Gulliver, travels to four different worlds. In one world, the people are very small, in another they are giants, and in a third, the country is ruled by horses. Most people today think of *Gulliver's Travels* as a children's story, like *The Voyages of Sindbad the Sailor*. In fact, *Gulliver's Travels* may even be based on the Sindbad stories. It is certainly true that millions of children have enjoyed the stories in simplified versions. But the author, Jonathan Swift, did not write the book for children. He wrote the stories as a criticism of the politicians in England, in particular, at the time of the war between Britain and France.

Robinson Crusoe is one of the most famous adventure stories in the English language. The hero, Crusoe, is shipwrecked on a desert island and lives there for 28 years before being rescued. The story, written by Daniel Defoe, is based on the true story of Alexander Selkirk, who spent three years on the uninhabited desert island of Juan Fernandez. It is now a popular story with children, but Defoe probably didn't write it as a children's book. Some critics say the story is an allegory for the fight between good and evil. I personally believe that Crusoe's life represents the advance of civilization from primitive society to modern life – at least, modern life in the 17th century.

Presenter: **D 2 Listen and check your answers.**
Female presenter:
a In Swift's book, the hero, Lemuel Gulliver, travels to four different worlds.
b *Gulliver's Travels* may even be based on the Sindbad stories.
c It is certainly true that millions of children have enjoyed the stories in simplified versions.
d But the author, Jonathan Swift, did not write the book for children.
e He wrote the stories as a criticism of the politicians in England at the time.
f *Robinson Crusoe* is one of the most famous adventure stories in the English language.
g It is now a popular story with children, but Defoe probably didn't write it as a children's book.
h Some critics say the story is an allegory for the fight between good and evil.
i I personally believe that Crusoe's life represents the advance of civilization.

Presenter: **Lesson 2: Listening**
A 3 Listen to the first part of the programme. Make notes.
Female presenter:
Jonathan Swift was born in Ireland on November 30th, 1667, the son of an English lawyer. He grew up in Ireland and attended college in Dublin from the age of 14 to 21. When he left in 1688, he became the secretary to Sir William Temple, an English politician. During the next 20 years, he worked as a secretary and as a priest in various situations. Clearly, this work gave him an insight into the worlds of politics and religion, and he started writing about these subjects. Incidentally, some people say that Swift married a woman called Stella Johnson around

1716. Others maintain that there is no proof of this. It is believed that Swift started *Gulliver's Travels* in about 1712, but he did not publish it until 1726. Apparently, readers of the day could recognise real people and events in the fictional characters and events in the book.

Swift wrote several other books, but nothing as important as *Gulliver's Travels*. He died on 19 October, 1745, aged 78.

Presenter: **B 2   Listen to the first part. Number in order the events in the yellow box.**

Female presenter: Let's hear part of the first story. Gulliver's ship is wrecked in a storm and he wakes up in the strange world of Lilliput.

Male reader: *When I awoke, it was just daylight. I tried to get up, but I was not able to move. I had fallen asleep on my back and I found that my arms and legs were strongly fastened on each side to the ground; and my hair, which was long and thick, was tied down in the same way. I felt other thin ropes across my body, from my chest to my thighs. I could only look upwards; the sun began to grow hot, and the light hurt my eyes. I heard a strange noise near me; but as I lay tied on the ground, I could not see anything except the sky. After a little while, I felt something creeping up my left leg, then over my stomach and onto my chest and up almost to my chin. Peering down, I saw a human creature no more than 15 centimetres high. He had a bow and arrow in his hands. Shortly, I felt more and more of the creatures until there were at least forty of them on my body. I was so surprised that I cried loudly and they all ran back in fear. Some of them, I was told afterwards, were hurt leaping to the ground.*
After a little while, I started struggling and managed to break the strings and wrench out the pegs which held my left arm to the ground. I dragged my head up, although the strings in my hair hurt me a lot. I was just able to turn my head about five centimetres. But the creatures fled a second time, before I could grab any of them. Suddenly I heard one of them cry aloud "TOLGO PHONAC" and in an instant I felt more than a hundred arrows like needles pierce my left hand.

Presenter: **B 3   Listen again and check your ideas.**
     [REPEAT OF EXERCISE B2]

Presenter: **C   Listen to the second part of the story.**
Female presenter: Eventually, Gulliver makes friends with the little people of Lilliput and learns their language. Then he finds out about the problems of the strange world.

Male reader: *One day, the king of Lilliput sent his friend, Reldresal, to see me. I put him on my hand so I could see him and hear him.*
'I have come' he said, 'to tell you about the problems in Lilliput. In our world there are two powerful countries. One is Lilliput, the other is called Blefescu. These two countries have fought a war for many, many years. It is all about eggs.'
'Eggs?' I cried. 'How can a war be about eggs?'
'It began as follows,' he replied. 'We always used to break eggs open at the big end before we ate them. Then one day the king's son cut his finger doing this, so his father decided that, in future, everybody should break open their eggs at the little end. Many

people disagreed with this law and fled from Lilliput. They went to the other great country, Blefuscu. Now the Big-endian exiles are so important in Blefuscu that the country has declared war on Lilliput. They are going to invade us any day.'
I was troubled. On the one hand, I did not think it was right that I should intervene in their war, but, on the other, the people of Lilliput had been so kind to me. I decided to end the war without bloodshed.

Presenter: **D 2   Listen to the third part of the story and check your ideas.**
Female presenter: Gulliver tells the king about his plans and then sets out to end the war.

Male reader: *The country of Blefuscu is an island situated to the north-east of Lilliput, from which it is separated only by a channel eight hundred metres wide. Of course, this is an immense distance for the little men, but nothing to me, for I am a prodigious swimmer. The whole fleet of Blefuscu lay at anchor in the main harbour, ready for the invasion of Lilliput. I made a strong cable and attached fifty hooks to it. Then I plunged into the sea, holding my cable with the hooks. I arrived at the fleet in less than half an hour. The enemy was so terrified when they saw me, that they leaped out of their ships, and swam to shore. I then took my cable, and, fastening a hook to the hole at the front of each ship, I began to pull the ships out of the harbour. While I was doing this, the enemy fired several thousand arrows, many of which stuck in my hands and face. They hurt me a lot but they could not seriously wound me. My only worry was my eyes and I had the sudden thought to put on my spectacles. When the people of Blefuscu saw their whole fleet moving away from the harbour, they set up such a scream of grief and despair as it is almost impossible to describe or imagine.*

Presenter: **E 2   Listen to the final part and check your ideas.**
Female presenter: What is *Gulliver's Travels* about? It seems at first to be a fantasy, with strange worlds and impossible creatures. Perhaps we could call it the first work of science fiction. But it is far more than that. It is an allegory of English politics of Swift's day. Perhaps it is an allegory of all societies in any age. Gulliver learns, in the land of the little people, that people argue and go to war over stupid things. In the second land, the giants live together without fighting, but Gulliver is tiny in that land. Does Swift mean humans are too small to understand? In the final land, Gulliver sees that humans can never learn to live together peacefully. It is a sad and bitter view of the world, from a man who was sad and bitter at the end of his life.

Presenter: **Lesson 3: Learning new skills**
     A 1   Listen again to the proper nouns. Write the words. Guess the spelling.
Voice: 1   Blefuscu
     2   Redresal
     3   Lilliput
     4   Swift
     5   Dublin
     6   Stella
     7   Johnson
     8   Jonathan
     9   Spencer

Presenter: **A 3 Listen again and check your spelling.**
[REPEAT OF EXERCISE A1]

Presenter: **B 3 Listen to some sentences from the story. Match the dramatic verbs with the common verbs in the blue box.**

Male reader: 1 After a little while, I felt something creeping up my left leg, then over my stomach and onto my chest and up almost to my chin.
2 Peering down, I saw a human creature no more than 15 centimetres high. He had a bow and arrow in his hands.
3 I was so surprised that I cried loudly and they all ran back in fear.
4 Some of them, I was told afterwards, were hurt leaping to the ground.
5 After a little while, I started struggling and managed to break the strings and wrench out the pegs which held my left arm to the ground.
6 I dragged my head up, although the strings in my hair hurt me a lot. I was just able to turn my head about five centimetres.
7 But the creatures fled a second time, before I could grab any of them.
8 I made a strong cable and attached fifty hooks to it. Then I plunged into the sea, holding my cable with the hooks.

Presenter: **Lesson 4: Applying new skills**
A 3 Listen to the first part of the programme. Make notes.

Female presenter: Daniel Defoe was born in London in 1660. His father, James Foe, was a butcher and candle-maker. It seems that the young Daniel was disappointed that he did not come from a noble family. Perhaps this is why he added *De* to his surname. *De* is French for *of*, and noblemen used it after their first names to say which lands they owned. Daniel Foe became Daniel of Foe overnight.
As a young man, Daniel was interested in politics, but eventually he went into business. When he was 24, he married Mary Tuffley. But neither Defoe's business nor his marriage was successful. By the early 1690s, he was involved in politics again, working secretly against James II, the king of England. He was caught and sent to prison. It may be that he decided in prison not to take sides any more. Certainly when he came out, he wrote for both sides of the political argument.
Late in his life, he took up writing fiction and produced a large number of adventure stories, although he did not publish all of them under his own name. His books were popular at the time, but only *Robinson Crusoe*, published in 1719, has become a classic work of English literature. Incidentally, Defoe did not make much money from his writing and, in fact, died a poor man in 1730.

Presenter: **B 3 Listen to the first part of the story. Number the items in the yellow box in the order that Crusoe finds them.**

Female presenter: Defoe's character, Robinson Crusoe, has many adventures before he is shipwrecked on his desert island. But most people only remember this part of the story …

Male reader: *When I woke up it was broad daylight, the weather was clear, and the storm had abated, so that the sea did not rage and swell as before: I was surprised to*

see that the ship was still afloat, stuck on a rock about two kilometres from the shore.
I resolved, if possible, to get to the ship, so I plunged into the water. But when I got there, I could see no way to get on board. I swam round twice, and the second time I spied a small piece of a rope, and by the help of that, hauled myself up into the forecastle of the ship; I found that she was holed, and had a great deal of water in her, but the stern was lifted up and everything in that part was dry. First I went to the bread-room and stuffed my pockets with biscuit, and ate it as I did other things, for I had no time to lose. Then I realised that I needed a boat to help me carry things back to the shore. We had several spare yard arms, and two or three large pieces of wood. I resolved to work with these, so I flung as many of them over board as I could manage for their weight, tying each one with a rope so it did not drift away; when this was done I slid down the ship's side, and pulling them to me, I tied four of them together at both ends as well as I could, in the form of a raft, and laying two or three short pieces of plank upon them cross-ways, I found I could walk upon it very well. What should I load it with? And how can I preserve it from the sea? I first got three of the seamen's chests, which I had broken open and emptied, and lowered them down upon my raft; the first of these I filled with bread, rice, three Dutch cheeses, five pieces of dried goat's meat, and a little corn. Next, I searched for and found tools to work with on shore. What about ammunition and guns? There were two very good rifles in the great Cabin, and two pistols, these I grabbed first, with some powder-horns, and a small bag of shot, and two old rusty swords; and now I thought myself pretty well freighted, and began to think how I should get to shore with them, having no sail, oar, or rudder…

Presenter: **C Listen to the second part of the story.**

Female presenter: Crusoe gets back to the shore eventually, but his problems are not over …

Male reader: *My next job was to view the country, and look for a proper place for my habitation, and where to stow my goods to secure them from whatever might happen; I had no idea where I was, whether on the mainland or on an island, whether inhabited or uninhabited, whether in danger from wild beasts or not. There was a hill no more than half a kilometre from me, which rose up very steep and high. I took out one of the rifles, and one of the pistols, and thus armed I struggled up to the top of that hill. I arrived after much difficulty and, to my despair, saw my fate. I was on an island surrounded on every side by the sea, with no more land to be seen except two islands, smaller even than this one, which lay about five kilometres to the West.*
I found also that the island was barren, and, as far as I could see, uninhabited, except presumably by wild beasts, although I could not see any. I did see a huge number of birds and when I shot at one which I saw sitting upon a tree on the side of a great wood, I believe it was the first gun that had been fired there since the Creation of the World.

Presenter: **D 2 Listen to the final part of the programme. What do some critics think the book is about? What about the presenter? Make notes.**

Female presenter:	What is *Robinson Crusoe* about? At one level, it is just an adventure story, and a very good one at that. But some critics have found a lot more in the book. Some say it is a rites of passage book with one man struggling to survive and, in the process, growing up. Others say there is more to it than that. At the beginning of the story, Crusoe is not a very nice person. Each time he sets sail, he is shipwrecked. Some say this is punishment for his sins. Finally, he arrives on his desert island. He builds a home and grows crops and raises animals. He eventually finds a man on the island and teaches him to believe in God. Finally, he wins several battles against natives who try to invade from nearby islands. I believe that *Robinson Crusoe* is the story of civilization told through the eyes of one man.
Presenter:	**D 3 Listen again. When the presenter pauses, predict the next word. Then listen and check.**
Female presenter:	What is *Robinson Crusoe* about? At one [PAUSE] level, it is just an [PAUSE] adventure story, and a very good one at that. But some [PAUSE] critics have found a lot more in the book. Some say it is a rites of [PAUSE] passage book with one man struggling to survive and, in the [PAUSE] process, growing up. Others say there is more to it than [PAUSE] that. At the beginning of the story, Crusoe is not a very nice [PAUSE] person. Each time he sets [PAUSE] sail, he is shipwrecked. Some say this is [PAUSE] punishment for his [PAUSE] sins. Finally, he arrives on his desert [PAUSE] island. He builds a home and grows [PAUSE] crops and raises [PAUSE] animals. He eventually finds a [PAUSE] man on the island and teaches him to believe in [PAUSE] God. Finally, he wins several battles against [PAUSE] natives who try to invade from nearby [PAUSE] islands. I believe that *Robinson Crusoe* is the story of [PAUSE] civilization told through the eyes of one [PAUSE] man.
Presenter:	**Theme 9: Sports and Leisure, Five Trillion Dollars per Annum** **Lesson 1: Vocabulary** **A Listen to a text about sport. Number the red words in the order you hear them.**
Female voice:	At one time, people who did sports were called sportsmen or sportswomen. At that time, an athlete was a person who ran races or took part in events on the field – for example, the high jump or throwing the javelin. Nowadays, people use the word 'athlete' to mean any person involved in sport. The word is used to separate the playing skills from the physical fitness of the player. So you will often hear someone say, 'He is a great tennis player and a superb athlete'. Athletes in any sport train hard and are very fit. They usually practise their sport for hours each day. Top athletes love to compete against other top players and, of course, to beat them.
Presenter:	**B Listen to a short text that contains the green words. Then complete the text with one of the words in each space. Make any necessary changes.**
Male voice:	Tourism is big business nowadays. The growth in travel for leisure has been enormous in the last half century, especially the increase in international holiday travel. For example, most people in Western Europe have now visited at least one other country, whereas 50 years ago only a tiny percentage of

	Europeans had been abroad. There are pros and cons to holiday travel on this massive scale. On the positive side, people learn about other cultures when they travel. Perhaps it is harder to go to war against a country that you have visited on holiday. On the negative side, tourism often has a big impact on the holiday destinations. Tourists sometimes destroy the things they have come to see. For example, visitors to the tombs in Egypt have damaged the old wall paintings with the flashlights of their cameras. Tourists sometimes turn parts of the foreign country into little versions of their own country. For instance, English tourism to Spain has led to Spanish shops and restaurants selling English food rather than Spanish. Why do people travel hundreds or even thousands of miles on holiday? Clearly, some want sun and sand, others want to see the ruins of an ancient civilization or just experience the lifestyle of a different culture. A lot of tourism is *sightseeing* – simply going to look at buildings or landscapes in a different country. Personally, I think most tourists just want to tell their friends later, 'I've been there, I've seen that and I've got the photographs'.
Presenter:	**Lesson 2: Listening** **B 3 Listen to the introduction. How does the lecturer answer the question?**
Male lecturer:	Welcome to the Faculty of Sports and Leisure Management. You are here today because you have chosen to study Tourism Management. Let me say straight away that I think you have made an excellent choice, for two reasons. Firstly, tourism is big business nowadays – we'll hear just how big in a few minutes. Secondly, it is important to study tourism because it is having a huge impact on many countries and areas of the world – a good effect in many cases, a bad effect in others. It is important to understand the impact of tourism because then we can begin to manage it correctly. So Tourism Management is an important and growing part of the massive global leisure industry. Before we look at tourism as a business and its impact on the world, however, we need to define the word. What exactly is 'tourism'? It is also useful to see how tourism started and how it has grown in recent years.
Presenter:	**C Listen to the introduction again and check your ideas.** [REPEAT OF EXERCISE B3]
Presenter:	**D 2 Listen to the first part of the lecture. Is the lecturer's definition similar to yours?**
Male lecturer:	One definition says that a tourist is a person who travels for pleasure, goes at least 50 kilometres from his or her home and stays away at least one night. Even this definition has been challenged. What about domestic tourism? This is where people visit tourist attractions in their own country and even their own town or local area and do not stay overnight. Perhaps there is only one key point about tourism – it is travel for pleasure. In other words, it is part of the ever-increasing leisure industry.
Presenter:	**E Listen to the second part of the lecture.**
Male lecturer:	International tourism on any scale is only about 50 years old. For people to travel for pleasure, they need time, money and good transport links. It is only recently that these three commodities have come

together for a large number of people in large parts of the world.

For thousands of years, most people hardly had leisure time at all. They worked, ate and slept. There were occasional holidays – the word 'holiday' in English comes, in fact, from 'holy day', so holidays were originally days for prayer and religious celebration. But even on these holy days or holidays, the majority of people had no money to spend on leisure activities. For the few wealthy people with time and money, transport links were so bad that it was no pleasure to travel anyway. Some people did make the effort, of course. Rich people from Britain and the States did the Grand Tour, visiting Rome and Athens and other locations from ancient history. Domestic tourism became more popular in England after the arrival of the railways in the 1840s. By the way, we distinguish between international tourism, where people go to another country on holiday, and domestic or internal tourism, where people stay in their own country. Seaside towns, in particular, started to cater for tourists in the summer. The first package holiday, which included transport by train, hotel rooms and food, was, apparently, organised by Thomas Cook in 1861. He arranged for a group of working men to go to Paris for six days. The package cost around two pounds per person.

Presenter:	**F 3 Listen to the third part of the lecture. Try to contribute to each discussion.**
Male lecturer:	So some ordinary people were travelling abroad on holiday by the end of the 19th century. But it is fair to say that there was very little international tourism until the 1950s. Indeed, the World Tourism Organisation, or WTO, estimates that in 1950 there were only 25 million international stayovers per annum worldwide. This may seem large until we compare it with more recent figures. I've given you a handout with a graph that shows the growth in world tourism over the last 50 years and an estimate for future growth. Can you find it? … What was the figure for total tourist stayovers in 1980?
Man 1:	Two hundred.
Male lecturer:	Two hundred what?
Man 1:	Million.
Male lecturer:	No, it's a bit more than that.
Man 2:	Three hundred million.
Male lecturer:	Yes, it's about 300 million, or perhaps a little less. What has it reached by 1990?
Woman 1:	Just over four hundred million.
Male lecturer:	Absolutely. And by 2002, the number had reached …?
Various:	Seven hundred and three million.
Male lecturer:	That's right. Actually, there's a slight dip in 2001. Why is that, do you think?
Man:	SARS?
Male lecturer:	No, that was later.
Man:	September 11th.
Male lecturer:	Yes. International terrorism can have a big effect on international tourism. For example, recently a very small country has been badly affected …
Man:	America.
Male lecturer:	No, I'm thinking of a small country that has seen a big decline in tourism because of terrorism …

Woman:	Bali.
Male lecturer:	Exactly. Anyway, back to the graph. The WTO has done an estimate of growth in international tourism in the next 15 years. When does it think the figure will reach one billion?
Man:	Two hundred and ten.
Man 2:	Two thousand and ten.
Male lecturer:	Yes, we can say two thousand and ten or twenty ten. The WTO estimates that the number will reach one billion in 2010 and 1.6 billion by 2020. And, of course, for every *international* stayover there are probably at least ten domestic stayovers. Domestic or internal tourism is also rising rapidly around the world. What is the financial value of this part of the leisure industry? I always ask my students this question at the start of the course, so what do you think?
Man:	A billion dollars?
Male lecturer:	Anyone else?
Man 2:	Ten billion dollars?
Male lecturer:	OK. Any other ideas? What about you? What do you think?
Woman:	I was going to say ten billion dollars.
Male lecturer:	OK. Well, actually, it is much, much more. According to the WTO, tourism contributes about five trillion US dollars each year to the world economy. That's a five and 12 noughts. That's about half the total annual production of the USA and about a sixth of the total annual production of the whole world.
	We can look at this huge figure another way. Tourism contributes about 16 per cent of the total world economy. How does tourism compare with other sectors? Well, agriculture contributes about four per cent to the world economy – so the industry that produces all the food in the world is about a quarter the size of tourism. What about petroleum? The industry that gives us most of our energy worldwide contributes about three per cent to the world economy, so tourism is five times bigger than the petroleum industry. In terms of employment, the World Travel and Tourism Council, or WTTC, estimates that, in 2003, the Travel & Tourism Industry will account for 195 million jobs worldwide, which is 7.6 per cent of total employment.
	Growth in this sector is also impressive. I've given you a block graph on this. As you can see, in Europe, tourism is growing annually at 2.9 per cent, while in the Americas it is nearly four per cent. What about in Africa? … Anybody?
Man:	Five per cent.
Male lecturer:	Well, it's a bit more than five per cent, isn't it?
Man 2:	5.5 per cent?
Male lecturer:	Yes, that's right. What's the figure for South Asia?
Woman:	Just over six per cent.
Male lecturer:	Right. But which region is at the top of the growth graph? What do you think?
Man:	Europe?
Male lecturer:	No, Europe's there already, isn't it? Any other ideas?
Man:	Japan?
Male lecturer:	Japan's in East Asia and the Pacific. Anyone else? … Come on, don't be shy.
Woman:	Is it the Middle East?
Male lecturer:	Absolutely. It's the Middle East, with an amazing seven per cent annual growth rate in tourism. This is

at a time when the world economy is only growing at about 2.8 per cent and many sectors are actually declining.

Now, I'd like you to work with the people near you for a few minutes. Think about this question. What are the pros and cons of tourism – the positive impacts and the negative impacts? Can you discuss that for a few minutes?

Presenter: **F 4 Listen to the third part of the lecture again and check your answers.**
[REPEAT OF EXERCISE F3]

Presenter: **Lesson 3: Learning new skills**
A 2 Listen and check your ideas.
Male lecturer: Let me say straight away
It is important to understand
It is only recently that
For thousands of years
The majority of people
It is fair to say that
We can look at this another way

Presenter: **B 2 Listen and check your ideas.**
Male lecturer: Before we look at tourism as a business, we need to define tourism.
Tourism has a good effect in many cases, a bad effect in others.
Even if you had time and money to travel, transport links were so bad that it was no pleasure to travel anyway.
According to the WTO, tourism contributes about five trillion US dollars each year to the world economy
In terms of employment, the travel and tourism industry will account for 195 million jobs worldwide in 2003.
Tourism is travel for pleasure. In other words, it is part of the ever-increasing leisure industry.

Presenter: **C 1 Listen to the next part of the lecture. Tick the points the lecturer mentions.**
Male lecturer: So tourism is big business. But what is the economic and social impact on a particular location? Let's imagine a small, sleepy fishing village, surrounded by rich farmland, miles from the nearest airport. There is not much employment in the village, but it has good weather and a nice sandy beach. People start to hear about the village and begin to visit it. Perhaps they are internal tourists. They stay in the one hotel in the village. The hotel has to employ more staff to look after the extra guests. The staff have more money to spend in the local community, which becomes more prosperous. As more tourists come, the hotel expands and the spiral begins to rise. Economists call this the Multiplier Effect, and it is the good side of tourism, the side that all national tourist boards try to encourage.

Of course, not all the extra spending benefits the local community. The hotel might import a lot of the food to meet the demands of the tourists, rather than purchasing it from the local farmers and fishermen. Economists call this leakage. And what about the jobs in the hotel and other parts of the tourist industry? Generally, jobs in tourism are unskilled and low-paid. There is demand for maids, waiters, cleaners, etc. As it gets bigger, the hotel might bring in people from outside the village, from another country even, because they are cheaper.

Again, there is leakage from the local community. There may be another negative impact of employment creation in tourism. People may leave the local production and extraction industries, like farming and fishing, to work in service industries – in the hotel itself and in restaurants and other tourist attractions that spring up. Eventually, some of the traditional sources of employment may die out altogether. The old fishing village surrounded by rich farmland may become a new tourist town with no room for fishing boats and nobody to work the fields.

Finally, there may be a social impact of the new jobs. Fishermen and farmers are very independent. They manage their own lives. If they become gardeners or cleaners, they may develop a different view of themselves. They may lose their self-respect.

There is another issue relating to different lifestyles. Tourists often do not have the same lifestyle as the locals. They demand different facilities, in many cases, including swimming pools and golf courses. Sometimes, facilities get better for everybody, including the local community. But often, tourists have priority over locals for the supply of water and electricity, and this can cause resentment and even do damage to other parts of the local economy.

Tourists spend money in the local community, and some of that will go back to the government in the form of tax, so the national government will benefit from local tourism. But this is not a complete gain either. Some of the taxation money must be spent on building the infrastructure for the new tourist industry. The old route to the fishing village is slow and the road is bumpy. The government has to build a new road from the airport, which, of course, has been expanded and updated. All of this costs money. In some cases, the cost of the infrastructure can be higher than the income from tourism. There is another effect of infrastructure – some of it is built on the beautiful land that the tourists came to see. This is the terrible irony of some tourism. Tourists may actually destroy the things they came to see and enjoy. A lot of tourism is sightseeing, but what if the sights are damaged by the tourists who have come to see them? A small, quiet, beautiful fishing village can become a noisy, busy, ugly tourist town.

The effect can be even worse where the environment is particularly fragile. Many tropical resorts, for example, are popular because of the coral under the sea very close to the shore. The rise of tourism in such an area can destroy the coral in just a few years. Firstly, souvenirs of coral become popular and both locals and tourists break off pieces. Secondly, ground up coral is a good building material. As more buildings go up, the coral reef goes down. Thirdly, the anchors of tourist boats scrape against the coral and damage it. Finally, the extra waste products from the growing town are piped into the sea and the coral dies under the murky waters.

What about the social impact on the original community? Tourism often divides local communities. Many in the community, usually the young, want the tourists to come, and like the changes that tourism brings. But others resent the way their community is changed by the tourists. I said at the beginning that the one certain thing about tourism is that it is travel for pleasure. When people go on holiday, they want to enjoy themselves, and this may mean that they behave differently from the way they normally do at home. They may also not understand or not care about the local values of the area they are visiting. The attitude of tourists can, therefore, have negative effects. Firstly, the local people start to resent the tourists. Secondly, they may see the tourists as representatives of the culture they come from. Travel, they say, broadens the mind, but travellers can set the minds of local people against them, with their rudeness and bad behaviour. Tourism may even contribute to terrorism, with resentment turning into hatred.

For all these reasons, tourism must be managed … and that's what you are here to learn about.

Presenter: **C 3 Listen to this part of the lecture again. Make notes of the extra points.**
[REPEAT OF EXERCISE C1]

Presenter: **Lesson 4: Applying new skills**
A Listen and check.
Voice 1: 1 economic impact
Voice 2: 2 internal tourism
Voice 1: 3 local community
Voice 2: 4 tourist industry
Voice 1: 5 different lifestyle
Voice 2: 6 swimming pool
Voice 1: 7 golf course
Voice 2: 8 electricity supply
Voice 1: 9 national government
Voice 2: 10 fragile environment

Presenter: **C Listen to each section from the second half of the lecture again.**
Lecturer: So tourism is big business. But what is the economic and social impact on a particular location? Let's imagine a small, sleepy fishing village, surrounded by rich farm land, miles from the nearest airport. There is not much employment in the village, but it has good weather and a nice sandy beach. People start to hear about the village and begin to visit it. Perhaps they are internal tourists. They stay in the one hotel in the village. The hotel has to employ more staff to look after the extra guests. What happens to the local community? Any ideas?

Of course, not all the extra spending benefits the local community. The hotel might import a lot of the food to meet the demands of the tourists, rather than purchasing it from the local farmers and fishermen. Economists call this leakage. And what about the jobs in the hotel and other parts of the tourist industry? Generally, jobs in tourism are unskilled and low–paid. There is demand for maids, waiters, cleaners, etc. As it gets bigger, the hotel might bring in people from outside the village, from another country even, because they are cheaper. Again, there is leakage from the local community. There may be another negative impact of employment creation in tourism. What do you think that could be? Another negative impact?

Finally, there may be a social impact of the new jobs. Fishermen and farmers are very independent. They manage their own lives. If they become gardeners or cleaners, they may develop a different view of themselves. Will the impact be positive or negative? What do you think?

There is another issue relating to different lifestyles. Tourists often do not have the same lifestyle as the locals. They demand different facilities, in many cases, including swimming pools and golf courses. Sometimes, facilities get better for everybody,

including the local community. But often, tourists have priority over locals for water and electricity supply. What is the social impact of this aspect? Tourists spend money in the local community, and some of that will go back to the government in the form of tax, so the national government will benefit from local tourism. But this is not a complete gain either. Why not? What is the negative side of tourism for national governments?

This is the terrible irony of some tourism. Tourists may actually destroy the things they came to see and enjoy. A lot of tourism is sightseeing, but what if the sights are damaged by the tourists who have come to see them? A small, quiet, beautiful fishing village can become a noisy, busy, ugly tourist town.

The effect can be even worse where the environment is particularly fragile. Can you think of a good example of a fragile environment that can be damaged by tourism?

What about the social impact on the original community? Tourism often divides local communities. In what way can tourism divide a community?

For all these reasons, tourism must be managed … and that's what you are here to learn about.

Presenter: **Theme 10: Nutrition and Health, Food – The New Poison?**
Lesson 1: Vocabulary
A Listen to some words.
Voice: meat
potatoes
eggs
palm tree
salmon
sheep
iron
vegetable
A, B, C, D and E

Presenter: **B Listen to two students doing the quiz.**
Student 1: What are you doing?
Student 2: This quiz on food hygiene.
Student 1: Oh, great. How are you doing?
Student 2: Well, I haven't started yet, really.
Student 1: Why not?
Student 2: I don't understand all the questions.
Student 1: For example?
Student 2: Well, Question 1, for a start.
Student 1: Question 1. *What makes food harmful?* What's wrong with that?
Student 2: What does *harmful* mean?
Student 1: It means it can hurt you, harm you, make you ill. I suppose they want you to say *bacteria*.
Student 2: What is *batkeria*?
Student 1: Bacteria. It means tiny, living creatures that you find in the air, or in water or, of course, in food. It's plural. *Bacterium, bacteria.*
Student 2: Right. Question 3. *Unsafe.* That's the opposite of safe, yes?
Student 1: That's right.
Student 2: So it means *dangerous*?
Student 1: Well, not as strong as *dangerous*, just not safe.
Student 2: OK. Question 5 – *store.* I thought *store* was a shop.
Student 1: It has two meanings. When it's a verb, it means: 'to keep for some time'.
Student 2: Right. Question 7 – *handling* comes from handle, is that right?
Student 1: Yes.
Student 2: Handle on a door?

Student 1:	No, *handle* as a verb. Touch with your hands. In this case, it means prepare, cook.
Student 2:	Oh, I see. OK, last one. *Defrost*. I suppose *de* means *not* or *un*?
Student 1:	Yes, that's right.
Student 2:	So it is the opposite of *frost*. I don't know that verb.
Student 1:	No, it's a bit strange. It's the opposite of *freeze*.
Student 2:	So *defrost* means 'unfreeze'?
Student 1:	Exactly.
Student 2:	Right. Now we can do the quiz …

Presenter:	**Lesson 2: Listening review (1)**
	B Listen to the introduction to the lecture. Complete the outline notes.
Male lecturer:	Today, I'm going to talk about food hygiene. I'm going to tell you about the factors that must be present for food to be harmful. There are three of them. They are bacteria, temperature and time. Then I'm going to talk about looking after food, which means, firstly, storing it correctly, and secondly, handling it correctly. Finally, I'm going to explain the importance of the use-by date on food.

Presenter:	**C Listen to the first part of the lecture and make notes.**
Male lecturer:	OK. So, first, when does food become harmful? There are basically three factors. Firstly, there must be harmful bacteria or microorganisms in or on the food. Microorganisms are tiny living creatures that are invisible to the naked eye. Actually, most bacteria are not harmful. In fact, the human body needs bacteria to work properly. But a small number of bacteria can cause illness and even death. The number of bacteria can grow very rapidly because they multiply. In other words, one bacterium becomes two, then four, then eight, and so on. Secondly, temperature. Bacteria multiply when food is between four and 60 degrees centigrade. This is called the Danger Zone for food. Below four degrees, bacteria cannot multiply or increase in numbers to a dangerous level. Above 60 degrees centigrade, most bacteria are killed. Finally, time. Bacteria need time to multiply, but not very much time. If we leave food in the Danger Zone for more than two hours, the bacteria can reach a harmful level.

Presenter:	**D Listen again and check your answers.**
	[REPEAT OF LESSON 2 EXERCISE C]

Presenter:	**E Listen to the second part of the lecture.**
Male lecturer:	How can you be sure that food is safe? It is impossible to be absolutely sure, because you cannot see bacteria. Some people think that food containing harmful bacteria always looks or smells funny, but this is not true. One very dangerous microorganism, which causes the fatal illness botulism, produces no changes in food that we can see or smell. But the vast majority of food you buy nowadays is safe, so if you store it correctly, handle it correctly and use it before the use-by date, you can be confident it is safe. However, there is a very simple rule about food. If you are not sure for some reason that food is safe, throw it away. In other words, if in doubt, throw it out! OK, so first you must store food correctly. Firstly, this means keeping fresh food in a refrigerator that is operating at the correct temperature – that is, below four degrees centigrade. It also means storing food correctly when you take it out of the refrigerator. Cover it to protect it from new bacteria, and don't

leave it standing for more than two hours. Finally, it means storing food correctly when you take it out of the house, for a picnic, for example. I remember once I went on a wadi trip and the host brought the food in shopping bags. There was meat and fish and eggs, all in the car in temperatures up to 40 degrees. We drove for about two hours. I didn't eat anything, but other people did and several of them had bad stomachaches the next day. Anyway, getting back to the point. Put food in a cool box and put ice in the cool box. A general rule is this: if there is still ice in the box when you open it, the food is safe to eat. So we've seen that we must store food correctly. Now let's consider handling food correctly. But what is the correct way to handle food? You must ensure that you don't transfer bacteria from your hands onto the food, so wash your hands before starting to prepare food. You must also ensure that you don't transfer bacteria from one piece of food onto another piece of food, so wash your hands after handling food. And remember to wash fresh fruit and vegetables before you eat them. There will be millions of bacteria on the surface, even though you can't see them.

Presenter:	**F 3 Listen to the third part of the lecture.**
Male lecturer:	Some people have called food 'the new poison', and it is true that food poisoning has increased all over the world in recent years. Why has food poisoning increased? Perhaps it is because people use modern household appliances wrongly in some cases. For example, the freezer is a wonderful invention that enables you to keep food like meat for several months without it going bad. The meat is quite safe in the freezer, but you must be very careful when you take it out to cook it. As you know, low temperatures do not kill bacteria, they just stop them multiplying, so when you take the meat out of the freezer, bacteria can start to damage the food immediately. You must defrost the meat in a safe way and then cook it for the correct time at the correct temperature. What is the correct way to defrost meat? What do you think? … Any other ideas? … Anyone else? Come on, don't be shy. … OK. The very best way to defrost meat is to put it in the refrigerator overnight. If you just leave the meat standing at room temperature, bacteria on the outside of the meat start to multiply before the inside of the meat has defrosted. If you defrost in a microwave, there might still be ice in parts of the food, and those parts will not cook properly and kill the bacteria.

What other modern invention causes problems with food hygiene? Well, the microwave is a wonderful invention, if it is used correctly. We can make hot meals in a few seconds. But are these meals safe? The answer is yes, if they have cooked properly all the way through, but you must turn food regularly in a microwave to make sure every part is cooked. With liquid foods, like soup, you must stir the liquid several times during cooking. Finally, what must you always do when you have finished cooking something in a microwave? Any ideas? … Anyone else? … What do you think? … Right. So, when you have finished cooking something in a microwave, you must leave the food to stand for a few minutes to spread the heat.

So to sum up. Most food that we buy in a shop is safe, but we must store it correctly and handle it correctly. There is one other thing we must do. I mentioned it at the very beginning. Does anyone remember? … We must eat it by the use-by date. That's the date printed on the top or the bottom or the side. Always check the use-by date, and if you have kept the food too long, throw it away.

OK, in the next lecture we are going to look at some facts and figures on food poisoning. We are also going to learn the Food Code, or how to be safe in the kitchen.

Presenter: **Lesson 3: Listening review (2)**
A 2 Listen and check your answers.

Voice: all over the world
cause and effect
for thousands of years
getting back to the point
in other words
it all started with
it is fair to say that
it is important to understand
it is only recently that
let me say straight away
on the one hand
so to sum up
the majority of people
the rest of her life
to put it another way

Presenter: **B 1 Listen again to parts of the lecture in Lesson 2. Find a good way to continue in the yellow box.**

Male lecturer:
1 Then I'm going to talk about looking after food, which means, firstly, storing it correctly, and secondly
2 There are basically three factors.
3 Actually, most bacteria are not harmful. In fact,
4 The number of bacteria can grow very rapidly, because they multiply. In other words,
5 If you are not sure for some reason that food is safe, throw it away. In other words,
6 Finally, it means storing food correctly when you take it out of the house, for a picnic, for example. I remember once
7 So we've seen that we must store food correctly.
8 Why has food poisoning increased? Perhaps it is because people use modern household appliances wrongly in some cases. For example,
9 So to sum up.
10 OK, in the next lecture

Presenter: **B 2 Listen to the way each part continues and check your answers.**

Male lecturer:
1 Then I'm going to talk about looking after food, which means, firstly, storing it correctly, and secondly, handling it correctly.
2 There are basically three factors. Firstly, there must be harmful bacteria or microorganisms in or on the food.
3 Actually, most bacteria are not harmful. In fact, the human body needs bacteria to work properly.
4 The number of bacteria can grow very rapidly, because they multiply. In other words, one bacterium becomes two, then four, then eight, and so on.
5 If you are not sure for some reason that food is safe, throw it away. In other words, if in doubt, throw it out!
6 Finally, it means storing food correctly when you take it out of the house, for a picnic, for example. I remember once I went on a wadi trip and the

host brought the food in shopping bags. Anyway, getting back to the point.
7 So we've seen that we must store food correctly. Now let's consider handling food correctly.
8 Why has food poisoning increased? Perhaps it is because people use modern household appliances wrongly in some cases. For example, the freezer is a wonderful invention that enables you to keep food like meat for several months without it going bad.
9 So to sum up. Most food that we buy in a shop is safe, but we must store it correctly and handle it correctly.
10 OK, in the next lecture we are going to look at some facts and figures on food poisoning.

Presenter: **Lesson 4: Listening review (3)**
B Listen to the introduction to the lecture. Complete the graph with the missing information.

Male lecturer:
Last week, we talked about food hygiene and I explained the importance of storing and handling food properly. After the lecture, several students came up to me and asked how important this subject really was. OK, they said, of course it was important to be careful with food, but you didn't have to go mad about it. After all, they didn't know anybody who had died from food poisoning. Surely, you just got a stomachache and that was that? Well, I'm pleased that your experience of food poisoning has not been too bad, but let me say straight away that food poisoning *is* a very serious danger, especially in a hot country, and you must constantly guard against it. OK, I hear you say, food poisoning is dangerous, but it isn't very common. It's true that it isn't the *most* common cause of accidental death. In most countries, that is road accidents. In the US, for example, they accounted for over 40,000 deaths in 2002. It isn't even the second most common cause, which is falls from ladders and high places. But it is the third most common cause of accidental death in the US, with nearly 10,000 deaths in 2002. That's nearly 11% of all accidental deaths in the country and more than drowning and fires put together. And in many countries, the trend is upwards, as more and more people store food wrongly in refrigerators and freezers, cook it wrongly in microwaves and keep it past its use-by date.

Presenter: **C 2 Listen again and check your answers.**

Male lecturer:
After the lecture, several students came up to me and asked how important this subject really was. OK, they said, of course it was important to be careful with food, but you didn't have to go mad about it. After all, they didn't know anybody who had died from food poisoning. Surely, you just got a stomachache and that was that? Well, I'm pleased that your experience of food poisoning has not been too bad, but let me say straight away that food poisoning *is* a very serious danger, especially in a hot country, and you must constantly guard against it. OK, I hear you say, food poisoning is dangerous, but it isn't very common. It's true that it isn't the *most* common cause of accidental death. In most countries, that is road accidents.

Presenter: **D Listen to the final part of the lecture. When the lecturer stops, predict the next word. Then listen and check your ideas.**

Male lecturer:	OK, so food poisoning is really [PAUSE] serious. You must protect yourself from food that is [PAUSE] unsafe. You cannot always tell that food is [PAUSE] unsafe from the way it [PAUSE] looks or the way it [PAUSE] smells. But there are ways to protect [PAUSE] yourself from eating unsafe [PAUSE] food. In the last lecture, I mentioned the most important [PAUSE] ones. But how can you [PAUSE] remember [PAUSE] them? I have devised a simple set of [PAUSE] rules. I call them the Food [PAUSE] Code. You just have to remember the four [PAUSE] Cs.

You must keep food [PAUSE] cold.
You must keep it [PAUSE] clean.
You must cook it [PAUSE] properly.
You must check that is has not gone past its use-by [PAUSE] date.